Christina Riggs is chair in the history of visual culture, Durham University, and a fellow of All Souls College, Oxford University. She is the author of six books, including *Unwrapping Ancient Egypt* (2014) and *Ancient Egyptian Art and Architecture: A Very Short Introduction* (2014).

CHRISTINA RIGGS

ANCIENT EGYPTIAN MAGIC

A Hands-on Guide

67 illustrations

 Thames & Hudson

Thanks, as ever, to Tom Hardwick for weighing the heart
of my Egyptology, and to Ben Hayes and Jen Moore at
Thames & Hudson, the former for convincing me to write
this, the latter for performing such effective magic over it.

First published in 2020 in the United States of America by Thames &
Hudson Inc., 500 Fifth Avenue, New York, New York 10110

www.thamesandhudsonusa.com

Library of Congress Control Number 2019940745

ISBN 978-0-500-05212-9

Printed in China by Shanghai Offset Printing Products Limited

CONTENTS

Introduction: A Box of Tricks 6

1 Magic Words 13

2 Princes, Priests, and Sorcerers 40

3 Dealing with the Dead 66

4 A Magical Menagerie 84

5 Oh, the Snake Bites... 116

6 Love, Sex, Babies 136

7 Predicting the Future 162

8 Magical Thinking 181

Further Reading 196
Sources of Illustrations 203
Index 204

INTRODUCTION

A BOX OF TRICKS

Sometime around 1650 BCE, in a tomb cut deep into the earth, an Egyptian magician was sent to the next life with the tools of his trade in this one: magic wands and figurines, and a box containing a bundle of reeds (spare pens) and his library of papyrus scrolls, in case he needed to check the exact wording of an incantation. Painted on the lid of the box was a hieroglyphic sign: a jackal stretched out on its belly, with its head high and ears alert. The sign meant 'secrets', perhaps labelling the contents of the box, or referring to the tomb-owner's profession – one of the titles given to Egyptian priests who specialized in reading, writing, and magic was 'master of secrets'.

Magic permeated the everyday landscape of life in ancient Egypt, but core to magic is its secrecy. Magic has to be mysterious in order to work. Otherwise, anybody could do it, and clearly not everybody can. If that might seem to dash the hope of trying out some ancient Egyptian magic, don't worry. Thanks to discoveries like the magician's tomb, we have a pretty good idea of how magic worked in ancient Egypt – and we can start to see why it mattered so much. The ancient Egyptians set great store by their magicians and the power of magic to make things happen. They had a word for magic – *heka* – and clear ideas about a magician's responsibility to use *heka* to help those who were unable to help themselves. Though that's not to say that magicians didn't get up to other tricks as well, as we know from ancient adventure stories telling tall tales of their exploits.

This book takes ancient Egyptian magic seriously by taking it on its own terms. Within these pages, you'll find spells to ease labour pains and headaches, spells for becoming invisible, and spells requiring magic wands, voodoo-dolls (sort of), and an Abracadabra. There'll be tales of fantastic beasts, secret chambers, and trips to the underworld, as well as tips for predicting the future. There will be a pinch of salt here and there; after all, the salt compound natron was ancient Egypt's best-performing detergent, and a crucial ingredient in mummy-making. Before we get carried away on a winged sun disk, though, let's first look in a little more detail at the magician's tomb, or what's left of it. That will help us understand what we mean when we talk about magic in ancient Egypt, and what the ancient Egyptians themselves thought magic could do – and who could do magic.

Mastering magic

When British archaeologists discovered the tomb shaft in the winter of 1895–96, they found that the two burial chambers at the bottom were empty of any inhabitant – no coffin, no mummy, and no hint of the occupant's name. The reuse of tombs at this time was common, and faithfully buried mummies often found themselves evicted in later years. Only the box of papyri and the objects found around it offered a clue to the original owner's identity. The shaft has become known as the 'Ramesseum tomb', because about four hundred years after the burial, a temple now known by that name was built above it in honour of King Ramses II (1304–1213 BCE). But it is also sometimes known as the 'magician's tomb', because of the objects found within.

This 3,600-year-old magician's kit contained a fascinating array of specialist equipment: wands made from curved hippopotamus tusks, incised with turtles, baboons, long-necked lions with wings, and knife- and snake-wielding demons; a bronze wand in the shape of a rearing cobra; and small figurines, including a lion and several baboons, one of the animals sacred to Thoth, the god of writing.

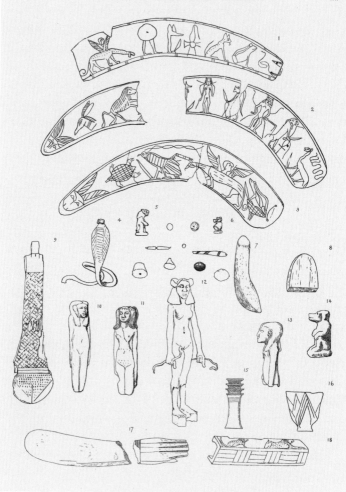

A magician's equipment? Line drawings of the magical objects
found in a box in the Ramesseum tomb.

There were beads and amulets, a little cup shaped like a lotus flower, and miniature models of food, including a melon or squash and a bunch of grapes. Three figurines in the form of naked women, made without any lower legs and feet, may have raised Victorian eyebrows at the time of the discovery. Similarly strange was a wooden statuette representing a naked woman whose face has the features of a lioness. She holds a miniature metal snake in each hand, resembling some of the figures incised on the ivory wands.

This collection of artefacts makes more sense the more scholars have studied similar material from around the same period, as well as the texts written on the scrolls found in the 'secret' box. Many of the objects found in the Ramesseum tomb show signs of long use, wear, and repair. The wands had been broken and put back together in ancient times, and the wooden statuette with snakes in its hands had been adapted at least once, perhaps to fit a new plinth. Any or all of these objects may have been heirlooms, made more precious and powerful by being passed down from one magician to another, until finally the decision was made to inter them in the tomb. Perhaps there was no one left to inherit them, or perhaps this particular 'master of secrets' wanted to take them with him. Who was going to argue with a magician, even after he was dead? Or especially after he was dead, since magic could even be used to move between this world and the next.

The box vanished at some point after the discovery, before the papyri and objects were divided between several museum collections in England, and the scrolls had been crushed, meaning that they have had to be painstakingly reconstructed from fragments. There are some secrets we'll never know. But there is quite a lot that we can piece together, like those fragmented scrolls. The papyrus was of the very best quality, and the texts were written in both hieroglyphic script and hieratic, a shorthand form of hieroglyphs that was easier and faster to use on papyrus. The box contained at least two dozen scrolls, representing a library built up over many years and perhaps handed down through generations, since, like many of the objects, some of the papyri had been reused and repaired over time. Among the many different texts written on them, there are hymns to the gods, ritual instructions for religious festivals, and classic works of Egyptian literature, including poems, adventure stories, and advice on living a good life. Magic spells predominate, though, from instructions for making amulets that can protect the body from harm to spells that call on the goddess Isis to help protect a house from any evil spirits that try to enter it. There are spells to ward off ghosts, snakes, and bad dreams; spells to drive away the demons that cause fever; and spells to guide a woman safely through childbirth and protect her newborn baby. Dealing with snakes, scorpions, and crocodiles was all in a day's work, and that's before we get to the ghosts and demons. You might still be baffled, for now, about the figurines of naked women or baboons, but perhaps you can start to see why a magic wand, or three, could come in handy.

Magic matters

A magician's methods were top-secret, but what magicians were capable of doing was common knowledge in ancient Egypt. And that takes us to the heart of why magic mattered. Magic was not just a show for entertainment, nor was it surreptitiously used to strike out against the people who were in charge in Egyptian society. In fact, magic was used *by* the people in charge. It belonged to gods, kings, and priests, the latter of which is what our 'master of secrets' almost certainly was.

If that seems surprising, it's because modern ideas of religious worship tend to treat religion and magic as if the two were opposites. Early scholars, like the archaeologists who found the Ramesseum tomb, considered religion a logical, orderly expression of belief in the divine, imposed on a populace and maintained by the top levels of society. They dismissed magic or witchcraft as mere superstition, a 'folk' practice that perverted higher ideas about divine presence by trying to influence and control divine power. Over the course of the 20th century, however, anthropologists and historians started to suggest other ways of thinking about magic. Among these was the proposition that if the people living in a given society themselves give great credit to magic and magicians, shouldn't we take those people at their word?

That's the approach that most Egyptologists take today, and it's certainly the approach you'll find in this book. By abandoning the attempt to categorize objects and practices straightforwardly as either 'magical' or 'religious', it becomes easier to consider magic in ancient Egypt from something closer to an ancient Egyptian point of view. Mysterious as magic was, it had its own logic and its own moral code. Through the work of priest-magicians, like the anonymous Ramesseum master, magic helped to maintain order in Egyptian society, whether that meant helping to settle disputes between neighbours, trying to heal the sick and reassure the worried, or, crucially, if more abstractly, keeping the cosmos in its correct alignment. The cosmos wasn't considered supernatural. Far from it: it was as natural as breathing, and sunrise, and birdsong, and it was all the more precious – and vulnerable – because of it. Magic was a way to protect the world and everything within it.

A distinctive feature of magic is that it tries to bring about an observable or tangible effect – a change that bends a little bit of the cosmos in the magician's favour. Some Egyptian magic had a clearly malicious intent, usually cursing an enemy, and some spells try to manipulate another person, such as bewitching a woman into falling in love. But the most common otherworldly intervention that most magic requested was simply a helping hand to survive. Life in the ancient world was tough, and most people had little control over their lives. They died of diseases we can cure with a pill today; families could be ruined by bad luck, or a blow to the breadwinner's reputation. But magic might be able to restore the balance when the odds were stacked against you by invisible enemies. The more extreme your problem, the more perilous the effort of addressing it might be. Therefore you needed someone equipped to deal with the potential danger of bridging the divide between the visible and the invisible, a specialist who was trained to see the unseen and to speak the secret language of the world's unfathomable forces. What you needed, in other words, was a little magic, and a magician to make it happen.

Magic could be used in the wrong way, too, of course – there was no doubt about that. Legal documents from the reign of Ramses III (*c.* 1175 BCE) show that one of his many wives plotted to have the king murdered, in order to manoeuvre her own son onto the throne. This conspiracy involved, as well as several government officials, at least five men who had knowledge of magic, according to their priestly titles. They were accused of using sorcery, magic potions, and wax figures to sway fate in the queen's favour – but the plot backfired, and most of the conspirators probably met painful deaths. But magic itself was not vilified; the problem was using magic against the king, the pinnacle of Egyptian society and a person who, like the gods, had his own deep resources of *heka* on tap.

In this hands-on guide to ancient Egyptian magic, you can try to tap into a little *heka* for yourself. There will be potions to brew, wax figures to enchant, and plenty of wordy, worthy spells to recite. At worst, you'll make a mess in the kitchen – or conjure someone up from the dead. At best, you can make yourself invisible and leave the cleaning-up (and the ghost) for someone else to deal with. Consider this a light-hearted look at a serious subject. Magic mattered to the ancient Egyptians, so it should certainly matter to anyone who has ever wanted to know more about them.

1

MAGIC WORDS

The phrase *djed medu* may not trip off the tongue, but it takes us to the heart of ancient Egyptian magic: speech. The expression, which translates literally as 'the words to be said', is used to mark the start of a spell in magic manuals. For all that magic needed special ingredients, and a magician who knew how to use them, it also required the right words, recited in the right way and under the right conditions.

There were three key components to any magic rite: a speech act, a physical gesture or action, and some kind of physical object that brought speech and action together. In ancient Egypt, words were powerful things, both in writing and when spoken out loud. The act of speech – to *djed* ('speak') the *medu* ('words') – was at least as important in practical magic as anything that was written down, painted, or carved in material form. But the spoken performances that brought alive the words written on papyri, artefacts, and works of art are impossible for us to observe from our vantage point thousands of years later. A little imagination helps – along with some judicious comparisons to other cultures around the world and over time, since some form of magic can be found in every society.

Magic supported the state, in the person of the king, and was at the heart of the religious rituals carried out in every temple, pilgrimage site, or household shrine up and down the Nile valley. Magic helped babies be born and the dead be reborn. It healed the sick, or tried to, and it offered some sense of calm and control when everything in the world seemed to be going wrong. The paradox is that while magical practices were part of everyday life, magic did its work by reaching beyond the everyday to access another realm entirely. We may have only silent objects to work with from the ancient past, or written instructions that seem obscure or incomplete. But ancient texts and artefacts help us build up a picture of how magic, and magicians, worked in ancient Egypt. From hieroglyphic inscriptions that hint at spells even older than the invention of writing, to wax figures that have melted away, much of our evidence for Egyptian magic can only ever show us the part of a rite that survives in some physical form. To hear the words that went with the rites would require time travel. For now, just read on with an open mind – we'll get to time travel in Chapter 2.

Talking the talk

Magic permeated every aspect of ancient Egyptian culture and every layer of its society. Starting at the top, there was nothing higher than the pyramids – and the kings who were buried in them. From the 5th Dynasty, elaborate hieroglyphic inscriptions covered the walls of the burial chamber and corridors deep inside the structure. These texts, which Egyptologists call the Pyramid Texts, are the oldest known religious texts in the world: they first appeared in the pyramid made for King Unas, who reigned around 2350 BCE. That doesn't mean that they were composed at this time, however. Their old-fashioned grammar indicates that these texts had much earlier roots, perhaps first having been written on materials that haven't survived, like linen shrouds or wooden coffins. The structure of the inscriptions offers another possibility: each fresh passage starts *djed medu*, which tells us that they were recited by a priest during the king's funerary rites. They may have been passed down through generations as an oral tradition, not unlike the poetry of Homer or the tale of Beowulf, before they were committed to stone inside pyramids.

Magic rituals for King Unas, carved inside his pyramid at Saqqara.

On the back of this mummy mask, each hieroglyphic text
begins with *djed medu*.

Egyptologists have published thousands of pages trying to translate and analyse the Pyramid Texts, whose language can seem obscure today, and was even archaic at the time they were first chiselled into walls. But they seem broadly to be poetic expressions with a magical force, aimed at ensuring the king's rebirth among the gods as a glorified being known in Egyptian as an *akh,* a sort of light-filled, eternal spirit. 'Recitation [*djed medu*]', starts a typical text from the pyramid of King Teti (r. 2323–2291 BCE), which continues: 'Greetings, Teti, on the day when you stand opposite the sun as it rises in the east, dressed in your finery as an *akh.*' On and on the texts run over the walls, elaborating a world of gods and divine blessings that await the dead king in the afterlife, as well as the dangers that he will have to overcome – with, of course, the help of magic.

Over centuries of Egyptian history, parts of the Pyramid Texts found their way out of the pyramids and into the tombs of Egypt's ruling classes and provincial leaders, in which they were often painted on coffins or other pieces of funerary equipment. The medium might have changed, but the method for activating their protective potential stayed the same; namely, a spoken performance by a priest-magician. The all-important act of reciting the right words in the right way was meant to help the deceased attain their desired end: eternal existence as an *akh.*

Although the context of these particular recitations was funerary, focused on ensuring the safe passage of the dead to the afterlife, we know that *djed medu* was an important part of other rites, too. The same phrase appears in the pictorial imagery that became standard on temple walls, for instance, and from there it found its way onto statues and other memorial monuments. A column of hieroglyphs next to a god or goddess often begins with *djed medu,* followed by the divinity's name. The words thus 'said' by Isis or Horus (to take two possible examples) had their magical potential made available for as long as the temples and monuments endured. Sometimes, where space was tight, only *djed medu* and the god's name would fit. Writing down exactly what the gods said seems to have mattered less than indicating that they would say something, forever – and that they would say it for you.

When it came to writing on scrolls of papyrus, scribes used a cursive script known as hieratic instead of the pictorial hieroglyphs we see on tomb and temple walls or painted and carved on works of art, like statues. Hieratic was easier and faster to write with the instruments available to scribes in ancient Egypt: a thin reed stem chewed at one end to make a brush, and two shades of ink, black made from carbon (charcoal) and red made from iron ore (also known as haematite or ochre). *Djed medu* and similar phrases were often written in red ink to mark the beginning of a new section of the text. In papyri devoted to magic spells or medical prescriptions (often one and the same), red marked lists of ingredients that needed to be gathered to perform the spell or mix up the recipe. Red lettering also gave the reader instructions as to what to do and say, or sometimes warned the reader of the need for secrecy, since some magic spells were so powerful that no one should be allowed to witness them. The incantations to be spoken out loud then followed in black. If you knew how to read and write in ancient Egypt – and very few people did – you understood this system of colour-coding, the same way we understand headings and paragraphs in a printed book.

Remembering just how limited literacy was in ancient Egypt is key to understanding its social structure, as is true of many other ancient societies. The best estimates are that only 2–3 per cent of the population could read and write. That percentage represents almost exclusively men of the upper echelons of the social hierarchy, who would have been schooled from childhood in both hieroglyphic and hieratic writing. That illiteracy was so widespread helps explain how religion and its counterpart, magic, were woven right through Egyptian life, from the top level of society down to its humblest members.

Being able to read and write hieroglyphs must have seemed like its own kind of magic to most people in ancient Egypt – the farmers and fishermen, weavers and market-stall sellers, craftspeople and labourers about whom so little survives in written records or works of art.

At the same time, we shouldn't over-emphasize writing as the only way to know or remember something. Certainly writing was important, and all the more so for being restricted to a small sector of society. But literacy isn't black and white (or black and red, for that matter). People who were not fully literate could still have had some grasp of common hieroglyphic symbols. Oral traditions were vital for learning, sharing information, and passing down knowledge, stories, and histories. Talking mattered, or else there would have been no need for those red-letter warnings to magicians, reminding them to protect their secrets from pricked-up ears as well as prying eyes.

What's in a name?

Magic and mystery go together like papyrus and ink, or poison and snakes. It may seem counterintuitive, but shrouding something in secrecy was a good way to advertise it. The more a magician could claim that only he knew what to do and how to do it, the more special his help would seem – and the more tempting his cure for what ailed you. In any case, every society needs secrets. Secrecy is a way to create, organize, and reinforce power, whatever form that power takes. Revealing or concealing secrets is effective at defining who is part of the 'in' group, as well as creating a sense of shared responsibility within that group, to use its secrets as a force for good.

In ancient Egypt, power over the natural and the supernatural spheres often came together in the world of the temple, its priests, and its libraries of written records, with the hallowed secrets they were said to contain. Ancient Egyptian myths grew out of this world and reflect the wider concerns of Egyptian society. Therefore it's no surprise to find secrecy featuring heavily in mythology, and especially in myths that involve the goddess Isis, who was often known by her soubriquet *Weret Hekau*, 'Great Lady of Magic'. One myth that explains how she came by her incredible talents gives us an insight into the power of both secrets and names.

Preserved in similar versions on several papyrus rolls dating from the 19th Dynasty (1292–1189 BCE), the story tells how Isis used her cunning and powers against the sun-god Ra. The sun was the central focus of Egyptian religion, but the sun-god himself took many forms and had many names – including a secret one. Isis encounters Ra in his doddering old age, before the nighttime journey that will see him born anew at dawn. She gathers some of the saliva dribbling out of his mouth, mixes it with clay, and shapes it into a snake. Using her magic, Isis transforms the clay model into a real snake and places it on the path along which the elderly sun-god is shuffling. The snake bites him, and venom begins to spread through Ra's already weakened body.

Isis appears in the nick of time, promising to use her magic to heal Ra, on one condition: that he tell her his secret name, which will make her the greatest magician in the world. Ra resists. Even to a fellow deity, he has no intention of giving away such a potent piece of information. As the poison reaches his eyes and strikes him blind, however, he relents. The secret name of the sun-god is...

Well, wouldn't that be nice to know. Unfortunately, some secrets are too sacred to commit to papyrus. According to the story, Ra's secret name passed directly from his body to hers, an ancient Egyptian mind-meld that made Isis the master of the universe where magic was concerned. Ra recovered to rise again the next day, even if we're still in the dark about the name he was hiding.

The name of a person captured something of their essence – or essences, plural; Egyptian gods, goddesses, and supernatural beings often appear under a dizzying number of different names and epi-thets. If a name is a powerful thing, after all, then having more of them can only be good news. Isis is a case in point. Her Egyptian name probably sounded something like *Aset,* the 's' at the end of 'Isis' having come to us through the ancient Greek spelling of her name. Egyptologists debate the meaning of the name *Aset,* which may have the same root as the word *was,* or 'power'. Whatever its origin, since *Aset* is written with the hieroglyph representing a throne, it seems to refer to Isis's role as a support for the king of Egypt: she is literally his seat, his place in the universe.

Isis was both the wife and the sister of the divine king Osiris, who ruled on earth in the days of the gods. His brutal murder by their brother, the usurper Seth, was one reason Isis needed to maximize her magic, the better to seek revenge and see her son Horus back on Osiris's rightful throne. Seth, the god of trickery, deception, and disaster, destroyed Osiris's body, some say by chopping it into pieces and scattering it throughout the land, and Isis had to travel far and wide, mourning her husband as she collected all the pieces of his corpse. Making the body whole again was the responsibility of the jackal-headed god Anubis, creating an origin-story for mummifica-tion. The cycle of myths around Osiris and Isis, Isis and Horus, and Horus and Seth forms the backbone to Egyptian magical practices. Almost literally, in fact, since the hieroglyphic sign for 'stability' (which, coincidentally, is pronounced *djed*) may represent the spine of Osiris. The matching symbol for Isis, called a *tyet,* was a knotted cloth the colour of blood. Its shape echoes the symbol for life, an *ankh* hieroglyph. Together Osiris and Isis, the *djed* and the *tyet,* combined the male and female elements needed for human creation, overcom-ing death to conceive their son Horus.

Isis then hid her young son in the Delta marshes, and raised him in secret, using her magical skills to protect him from the perils there. Only when Horus reached adolescence and manhood could

Alternating *djed*-pillars and *tyet*-knots on the largest burial shrine
from the tomb of Tutankhamun.

he challenge Seth, sparking off a series of battles and confrontations between uncle and nephew. Ultimately, a council of gods declared Horus triumphant, and in his falcon-headed form, he was hailed as the avenger of his father's murder and the rightful heir to the throne of Egypt. Osiris himself stayed firmly put in the Duat, presiding over the judgment of new arrivals and daily reigniting the sun's fire to maintain the cycle of cosmic renewal. Stories and spells place more emphasis on Osiris in matters of mummification and burial, and on Isis and Horus when it came to everyday concerns like health; together, Osiris, Isis, and Horus are a mythological theme that runs right through Egyptian magic.

Isis certainly put her own hard-won magic to good use. Her title Great Lady of Magic, *Weret Hekau*, shows that not only did Isis have magic, she had it in spades: the spelling puts *heka* in its plural form, *hekau,* which English can't easily convey ('magics'). The concept of *heka* is older than the pyramids; in the Pyramid Texts, heaven groans and the earth trembles in the presence of *heka,* the force – the magic – that impels the creation of the world. In this cosmic sense, magic is older than the gods, and even has more power than they do. As we saw in the story of Isis and Ra, gods need magic. They thrive on it, and it was by calling on divine beings like Isis that Egyptian magicians could seek to harness a little bit of *heka* for their own use on earth.

Perhaps Ra's secret, magic-giving name was just that, *heka,* a simple expression of a powerful concept. Some ancient Egyptians actually wound up with *heka* in their personal names; names such as Hekawy, Hekaf, or just plain Heka are attested from early times. Although some Egyptian names can seem incomprehensibly long to us today – Nesitanebtisheru, to take one tongue-tripping example – that is in part because they mean something. That particular mouthful, for instance, would have been given to a baby girl to honour the goddess Mut. It means, literally, 'She belongs to the Lady of Isheru', *isheru* being a sacred, artificial lake associated with this mother-goddess at the vast temple complex of Karnak in present-day Luxor. Many Egyptian names refer to gods or goddesses, perhaps as a way of placing people under the care of that deity. *Heka* even came to be worshipped as a god in later periods of Egyptian history, which may be why some men living around 600 BCE were named Hekaemsaf, 'Magic is his protection'.

Names mattered a great deal in Egyptian society and in the performance of Egyptian magic. What did it mean, then, that the dead were often called by the name of the god Osiris in addition to their own? In the Old Kingdom, when the Pyramid Texts were inscribed in royal burials, the dead king was identified with Osiris. Since Osiris had once been a king, that made mythical sense. Soon enough, privileged but non-royal men such as state officials, provincial governors, and important priests were compared to Osiris, too. By the New Kingdom, in the burials of men of status, we find the dead addressed as 'the Osiris so-and-so [the dead person's name]', or perhaps (the grammar is ambiguous) 'the Osiris *of* so-and-so', as if the blessed dead had an Osiris-form among all their other spirit manifestations. It wasn't too long – only a few centuries – before some women, too, were being addressed as 'the Osiris' on their coffins or in their Book of the Dead papyri, but later they were more commonly referred to as 'the Hathor', using the name of the goddess most closely associated with cemeteries and the western horizon, where the Duat began. A name had great power and captured something unique and essential to you, so in the right mouth, it could be a blessing – but in the wrong one, a curse.

Curses fit for kings

Magic words and actions were often a force for good: Isis wanted to increase her magical powers to help protect her son Horus from danger, which made her especially popular among anxious mothers.

Most magic spells were concerned with healing the physical body, or helping its spirit cross into the next world and flourish there, like the Pyramid Texts that prepared King Teti for a cosmic dawn. But ancient Egyptian magic had its dark side. Magic had to be able to handle danger, because the world is full of danger. Whereas today we would class these dangers – critical illness, destructive weather, armed violence – as either natural or man-made phenomena, to be counteracted with natural or man-made means, in the ancient world these were seen as threats to the cosmic order of the world itself by forces both known and unknown, visible and invisible, and must be counteracted by similarly mysterious means. Magic that had the power to counteract these otherwordly forces must be very powerful indeed – and thus could be a dangerous thing itself.

Cursing named individuals, or more often entire groups of people, is one of the oldest types of Egyptian magic. It's a form of magic that relied on the power of names, combining written and spoken words in a ritual designed to curse – effectively, to kill – people who were considered some kind of threat. A threat to whom, you might reasonably ask, and the answer may be surprising. These dark rites weren't harmless hocus-pocus carried out by your local wizard to settle some private grudge (although certainly that had its place in neighbourhood feuds). Rather, the people on the receiving end of these ritual curses were the enemies of Egypt itself, and found themselves the targets of the most powerful, state-sponsored magic.

Geography shaped the river landscape that comprised ancient Egypt (known by the Egyptians themselves as *Kemet*), and during the major periods of political centralization – the Old, Middle and New Kingdoms – the Nile valley from the First Cataract in the south to the Mediterranean coast in the north seem to have been united under a single ruler. But ancient territories are not the same as the modern idea of a nation-state, with fixed boundaries drawn onto maps in solid lines, and at various times this territory included several oases in the western desert, stretches of coast up into Palestine and the Levant, outposts on the Red Sea and the Sinai peninsula, and regions south of the First Cataract that extended, at times, into modern Sudan. In the north of the country, the Delta was rich with settlements, agricultural land, and travel routes, but very little evidence has been preserved there in a way that archaeology can find it. A ruler's territory was as big as he (sometimes she) cared to claim it was, and who did or didn't count as an Egyptian was often in the eye of the beholder. Threats to the royal authority, of course, could also come from within.

With their knack for giving dull names to interesting things, Egyptologists refer to the ritual curses against Egypt's enemies as execration texts. The magic objects on which they are inscribed are execration figures, 'to execrate' being a rather old-fashioned English word for the formal act of laying a curse. Made of clay, wax, Nile mud,

Limestone figure of a bound prisoner,
for use in curse spells.

or sometimes stone, execration figures represent prisoners with their arms pinned behind their backs and often tied together; some are rectangular plaques only just recognizable as human forms. The more elaborate figures often wear loincloths and have perforations where hair or beads would have been attached. Some figures seem to represent people deemed 'foreign' in the dominant Egyptian worldview, whether they were from lands beyond the Delta and the Nile valley or minority groups living in or passing through Egyptian territory. The curse texts written directly onto these figures, or on the pots and boxes in which they were placed, name people with both Egyptian and recognizably non-Egyptian names, but it's worth remembering that a name is only one aspect of an individual that might mark social difference.

One pottery vase used in this curse ritual has an inscription inked on its side, giving the personal names and family trees of five rulers from Kush, an area that covered what is now southern Egypt and northern Sudan. Also known as Nubia, this region was important to the Egyptian state as a source of gold, ebony, ivory, and other exotic products that were traded along the southern reaches of the Nile and across the Sahara and Sahel. The vase also names some thirty rulers from the eastern edges of the Mediterranean, where Israel, Jordan, Lebanon, and Syria now lie. 'Asiatics' is the generic term applied to peoples from these areas in Egyptology, a hangover from when this part of the world was referred to as Western Asia. Together, Asiatics and Kushites were the stereotypical villains for Egyptian pharaohs, much like Soviet agents in a classic James Bond movie.

The curse text on the vase makes it clear what a threat these enemies posed, and what would happen to them if the curse worked:

If they or any of their allies, courtiers, or confederates
will rebel, plot, fight, or even consider fighting or rebelling,
in fact, if any people, anywhere in this country, will fight

or consider fighting or rebelling, they will suffer every evil
word, recitation, thought, plot, struggle, disturbance, every
evil thing, every nightmare in a terrible slumber.

This text, together with the long list of names, may reflect what
the magician had to recite as he performed the actions associated
with the curse ritual. Like so many magical acts, this wasn't something that could be thrown together quickly. Execration rituals were
sometimes performed on a grand scale. At the Egyptian fortress of
Mirgissa in Nubia, which may have helped control trade in this region,
a pit 2 metres (6½ feet) wide and 70 centimetres (27½ inches) deep
contained the fragments of more than 700 intentionally smashed
pots, many of them inscribed with an execration text similar to that
above. A few metres away, a second pit contained, amid the melted
remains of wax execration figures that had been tinted red, a decapitated human skull; the rest of the skeleton was found in a shallow
grave nearby. A third ritual deposit, at a further remove from the first
two pits, held four limestone statuettes that were also inscribed with
curses, although only two of the statuettes survived intact because
of the damage inflicted on them before they were buried.

The rite carried out at Mirgissa, around 1800 BCE, was obviously
a complex ritual event involving lengthy preparation. Not only did
the pots, the red wax figures, and the limestone statuettes have to
be made and, where necessary, inscribed, but they then had to be
ritually broken, trampled, and melted, not to mention buried in the
three different pits. This particular ritual also included an execution,
to judge by the decapitated human remains. Given the strategic
importance of the fortress, on Egypt's southern frontier, it may well
represent a state-sanctioned ritual, with a prisoner sacrificed to set
an example and strengthen the curse's effect.

Cursing an enemy was clearly a practice fit for a king, whose role
on earth was to uphold justice and order. But not every execration

rite was carried out on such a scale. The practice was much more widespread, and easily adaptable to different contexts, whether under official sponsorship of some kind or undertaken for more personal motivations. Most curse deposits, which might contain just a few figures, have been found in cemeteries, perhaps taking advantage of the privacy this setting afforded – and its liminal status between the natural and supernatural worlds. Curse rituals were also performed in temples. And curses could get very personal, judging by the range of individual names, including women's names, that were inscribed on execration figures. Were curses used to settle private scores, if an offense had cut deeply enough to warrant such an action? It's difficult to know for certain, but it's certainly the case that in ancient Egypt, words could harm as well as heal.

Knotty problems

The spells and objects used in execration rites can help us understand the frequent representation of enemy figures in ancient Egyptian art, with their bodies bruised and their arms and legs lashed together. Bound prisoners appear in an astonishing array of contexts, starting from a period before writing even existed. These prisoners represent the enemies of the all-powerful king of Egypt, who is inevitably shown as the hero of scenes where he bashes them over the head while grasping them by the hair. But these bound, cowering captives represent much more than literal prisoners or actual military foes. They are the forces of disorder that threaten *maat*, the Egyptian concept of cosmic order and justice, in which the king's position as the uniting figure at the head of society was all-important. Pinioned enemies also threaten the eternal existence of the blessed dead, who trample them underfoot on painted mummy cases from the time of Cleopatra.

King Narmer grasps a mace to strike an enemy – the 'smiting scene' that symbolizes royal triumph over disorder.

Trampling or grinding something into the ground was one of the actions called for in curse rituals, as we've seen. So too was the act of binding itself. By subduing and controlling the threatening force or person, knotting also had a positive role to play in magic. Many spell manuals instruct the magician to recite the words while creating a knot in a length of cloth. The cloth was always linen, and some spells even specified a particular variety or grade. Linen was the main textile product of ancient Egypt, and was rich with symbolic values. As a plant, rather than animal, product, it had a meaningful link with the agricultural cycle and, by extension, nurturing new life from bare earth. Only bleached, or at least undyed and thus pure, linen was used in religious rituals, including the mummification of humans and animals. In the daily rites carried out in every temple in Egypt, priests – themselves dressed in fresh linen – wrapped the 'bodies' (that is, the statues) of the gods, kept in special shrines inside the sanctuary, in new clothing, which would be removed and replaced in the same ritual the next day. The clothes of the gods were, of course, clean, fresh linen, the best of which, called royal linen, was a product of workshops attached to the temples themselves.

The ancient Egyptian word for a knot, and for tying a knot, was *tjes*, and by tying a knot in a strip of linen, a magician could create a very simple but effective amulet to help someone in difficulty. Knotted cloths with magic drawings on them, made while magic words were spoken over them, were used for healing and protection. The magician made a series of knots, one after another, with each spell he spoke, so that the knot captured their effect. The number of gods drawn on a strip of cloth corresponded to the number of knots, as if each god's protective power was, like that of the incantations, being 'locked' into the linen. The patient would then wear the knotted amulet around his or her neck, or apply it to the affected body part if healing was required. Among the recommendations for stopping a miscarriage, for instance, was a spell to be recited while knotting a length of cloth, which was then to be inserted into the vagina. This may seem like a useless, even dangerous, remedy from our point of view today, but the gesture perhaps gave some hope or strength to the suffering woman, even if nature took its inevitable course. Knotting a cloth around someone's head, like a bandana, may also have been a form of healing or protective magic. In tomb or coffin paintings that represent funerals and other religious rites, some of the people involved in the ritual wear such headbands as if to signal their status, but the bands may also have conveyed protection during the work that a ritual performance involved. More prosaically, a textile anointed with herbal ointment and enlivened with magic words tied gently around the forehead was a prescription for headache relief.

Knotting magic made use of materials other than linen, too. Lengths of thread, yarn, and even hair could be knotted as part of a magic rite, and knotted linen or cord is sometimes found in conjunction with a textual amulet written on a strip of papyrus.

A papyrus amulet with magic spell and crocodile drawing, which would have been folded up small and worn on a string for protection.

Instructions for creating these papyrus amulets specify that the scribe either draw or write certain images or words on a piece of fresh papyrus – that is, papyrus that hadn't been used before, as scribes often recycled sheets of papyrus by rubbing over and erasing earlier texts. Since the ancient Egyptian language uses the same word for both 'to draw' and 'to write' (*sesh*), what appears on the papyrus amulet varies from drawings of different gods and animals to entire spells dutifully copied, instructions and all. The strip of papyrus was folded several times into a tight, tiny bundle that was then tied to the knotted linen or cord and worn around the neck for a double dose of magical aid.

The hieroglyphic symbol for an amulet, *sa*, was itself an oversized knot, representing a bundle of reeds folded into a loop and lashed together at the ends, perhaps to make a simple life preserver for people working on or near the Nile (ancient Egyptians don't seem to have been proficient swimmers). *Sa* meant 'protection', which was exactly what amulets were meant to do – protect you from any danger or malice that might come your way. And if hearing the magic words spoken out loud didn't quite convince you, turning them into wearable hieroglyphs just might.

Spelling it out

Like the *tyet* associated with the goddess Isis, several Egyptian hiero-glyphs that represent knots were used as protective devices, either as patterns in the decoration of objects and buildings, or as amulets that could be worn by the living or placed on the bodies of the dead. The *tyet* echoes the shape of the best-known Egyptian hieroglyph, the *ankh*. Some Egyptologists have proposed that the *ankh* represents the strap of a sandal seen from above, perhaps associating it with the ability to stand up and walk, but like the *tyet* it may simply represent an amuletic knot, with a loop at the top and short projections to the sides. In the Egyptian language, *ankh* meant 'life' or 'to live', making it a very powerful symbol indeed. Gods and goddesses are often shown holding an *ankh* in one hand, while the name of a king was always followed by the expression *di ankh* ('given life') and sometimes *ankh wedja seneb* ('life, prosperity, health'). This honoured and protected the name when it was written or spoken out loud. *Ankh* was also the word for a mirror, and some mirrors were made in the shape of the *ankh* hieroglyph – the Egyptians appreciated the opportunities for wordplay that their pictorial script afforded them. Mirrors were discs of polished bronze, which corresponded neatly to the loop of the *ankh* and recalled the shape of the sun, itself a hieroglyph for the sun-god Ra.

Another hieroglyph that represents a knot – in this case a knotted rope or cord – is the *shen*. As a verb, *shen* meant 'to encircle', but it also implied protection. The act of wrapping a cloth or a cord around something was a form of protection, after all, rather like building a protective fence or enclosure wall. Tying a knot also entailed circling one end of a cord around another, creating layers of circling actions. As a symbol in Egyptian art, the *shen* glyph also implied eternity; they are held in the talons of deities represented as birds, or offer support for figures of the gods or expressions of time. The symbol that Egyptologists call a cartouche, used to encircle the names of kings, is an elongated *shen*. As we saw in the myth of Isis and Ra, names held the essence of a person. They needed protection as much as a person's body did – and all the more so when that person was the king, whose names (most kings took four new names when they ascended the throne) and body represented Egypt itself.

The discovery that individual hieroglyphs, or groups of hieroglyphs, were used widely as both amulets and emblems at first invited some head-scratching among archaeologists. If only a tiny fraction of the population in ancient Egypt could read and write, were these

Mirror case from the tomb of Tutankhamun, in the form of an *ankh*, the hieroglyphic sign used to write both 'life' and 'mirror'.

The cartouches of King Horemheb, from his tomb in the Valley of Kings.

symbols lost on them? In fact, there's no reason not to assume that Egyptians outside of educated circles could also understand the names and meanings of hieroglyphs used in amuletic or emblematic ways. Having a glimpse of this knowledge may even have added to the overall sense of the magical potential that writing offered. Remember, too, that there were visible and functional differences between the full, pictorial form of hieroglyphic writing used in art and formal inscriptions and the cursive forms (hieratic and, in later periods, Demotic) that were more commonly used to write stories, spells, letters, and legal documents on rolls of papyrus.

The pictorial form and general inscrutability of hieroglyphs, however, encouraged many people in and beyond Egypt to think of them in mysterious, mystical terms. It was an attitude that Egyptian priests encouraged, composing ever more cipher-like inscriptions in the temples built during the era when the country was under first Greek and then Roman rule. To Greek and Roman visitors, starting with the historian Herodotus in the 5th century BCE, Egyptian priests emphasized the sacred character of hieroglyphic writing and the secrets it concealed. This played very well in the increasingly interconnected Mediterranean world, and Egyptian priests gained a reputation for magic and wisdom that earned them either grudging respect or sardonic smirks, depending on whether or not one believed in their powers.

The more specialized hieroglyphic writing became, the more esoteric and fascinating it seemed. The last dated hieroglyphic inscription is found in the temple of Philae, on an island in the Nile near present-day Aswan, written in 394 CE to honour the goddess Isis. Probably in the same century, an Egyptian priest named Horapollo wrote a guide to hieroglyphs that only added to their mystique, offering some rather convoluted explanations for the meaning of different signs. When a manuscript of Horapollo's book resurfaced in a Venice-controlled part of Greece in the 15th century and was taken to Florence, it caused a stir among Renaissance scholars and made Europeans hungry to decipher the script, which they were sure held the secrets of the universe. In the Arabic-speaking world, meanwhile, scholars such as Ibn Wahshiyya, who lived in the 9th century ce, might have been able to read hieroglyphic inscriptions to some extent. Many Islamic scholars were in awe of the accomplishments of Egypt's earlier inhabitants, with their pyramids, treasure-filled tombs, and picture-writing; they had read Horapollo, too, and accepted the symbolic power of hieroglyphs.

The ancient Egyptians themselves recognized that there was magical potential in hieroglyphic signs, in part because of their pictorial nature: if a hieroglyph represented a poisonous viper, it could potentially *be* a poisonous viper, like the clay snake that Isis made and brought to life in order to poison (and then save) the sun-god. All images, including hieroglyphic signs, had magical potential, for good or for ill. This seems to have been a premise of ancient Egyptian thought, and its logical conclusion meant that some images were put out of commission on purpose, to be on the safe side. In a hieroglyphic inscription, for instance, that viper symbol might be painted or carved in two distinct halves, to render it incapable of action.

The power of hieroglyphs echoes the power of language itself. Almost by magic, we've come full circle to the *djed* part of the phrase *djed medu* that opened this chapter: the act of saying something out loud. Make as many clay snakes as you like, but without the appropriate incantations, they will never come to life. The spoken word was crucial to Egyptian magical practice. Magic words made magic work, even if – as in the Pyramid Texts – those words were turned into formal prose and literally carved in stone. There was magical potential in the very words used to refer to certain things, gods, or people, as we saw with the story of Isis and the secret name of the sun-god Ra. The actions that accompanied the words mattered, too. Breaking or trampling on the so-called execration figures was a vital part of the curse rituals meant to destroy the real or imagined enemies of Egypt. Positive, protective magic had its own actions, such as the knots that served as amulets or surrounded kings' names. Circling each end of a cord around itself, to tie a knot, also 'tied' the incantation into the strip of cloth or papyrus.

We might also imagine that how a magical incantation was spoken was as important as the words themselves. When it came to pronouncing the words that made magic happen, a magician might have needed to change his or her tone of voice, or make sounds that probably weren't found in everyday speech, such as hissing, growling, clicking the tongue, or popping the lips. Magic wasn't something just anyone could do; nor was it something you could learn simply by reading a book (except for this one, of course). Who got to be a magician, and how they went about it, takes us to our next chapter. So if you are reading this on papyrus or an eReader, scroll on. Otherwise, turn the page.

Sir Edward Poynter's 1881 drawing of the Biblical scene where
Moses and Aaron confront the magicians of pharaoh.

2

PRINCES, PRIESTS, AND SORCERERS

To many people today, the most familiar example of an Egyptian magician is Moses. Yes, that Moses, the Old Testament prophet who led the Hebrews from servitude in Egypt to freedom in the promised land of Canaan, giving us the Ten Commandments along the way. For centuries, there was no conflict between the magical prowess of Moses and his role as a wise prophet. Not only was Moshe or Musa ('Moses') called upon in Jewish and Christian magic spells into the medieval era, but he features as a sage in the Quran as well. The Book of Exodus tells us that Moses was raised as an Egyptian, and a privileged Egyptian at that. His Jewish birth mother floated him in a basket in the Nile marshes when he was just a baby, to save him from a pharaoh who ordered all the male children of the Hebrews killed. When pharaoh's daughter found him, she gave him his Egyptian name ('Moses' comes from the verb 'to be born') and brought him up as her own son. Only as an adult did he realize his true origins. Witnessing the terrible treatment of a Hebrew slave, Moses struck and killed an Egyptian man, then fled the country to escape the punishment of pharaoh, his adoptive grandfather. So much for life as an Egyptian prince.

Exodus is first and foremost a story of how the Hebrew god Jehovah used Moses to save the Jewish people from Egyptian oppression. But it is also brimming with tales of ancient magical practice. With his brother Aaron for support, Moses returned to Egypt and secured an audience before the king of Egypt, by that time a different ruler from the pharaoh of Moses's youth. Show us a miracle, said pharaoh. So Aaron held out a rod and threw it to the ground, where it instantly turned into a snake. The king called his own sorcerers forward. What did they think of this miracle? Not very much, because they knew the same trick. The ground in front of pharaoh soon writhed with reptiles as each of his magicians threw down a wand, only for Aaron's serpent to eat up the newly sprung snakes, one by one.

Ancient Egyptian literature provides several precedents for this magical confrontation between serpent-wielding sages. Magicians often play a central role in Egyptian tales that combined history, adventure, humour, and moral instruction, and which today give us an important insight into the high status that magicians held in Egyptian society, and how these priest-magicians themselves liked to be seen. Being a magician was a big responsibility. Having magical powers at your disposal could place you at a king's right hand, but magic could also get you into trouble if not used wisely. Skilled magicians could fly like birds or make themselves invisible, according to the spells we know they had at their disposal. More importantly, they held positions of trust in their communities, helping people at times of crisis and need. Magic wands shaped like serpents really did exist, with a real purpose: to keep dangers at bay in a dangerous world.

Magic at the royal court

Egyptian magic started at the top with the king himself. The Pyramid Texts – those ancient written versions of even older incantations – describe the king as *hekau*, 'possessor of magic'. Rather than implying that the king performed magic, this seems to suggest that the king's whole person had magical qualities. He was, after all, more than human, thanks to his unique relationship with the gods. The servants who came into close contact with the king – such as his barbers and manicurists – had to be equipped, magically, to handle the *heka* that existed in his body. Shaved-off stubble, hair trimmings, and nail clippings contained some of that magical force and therefore had to be disposed of safely; in the wrong hands, their *heka* could wreak havoc. No wonder some of these servants earned themselves fine tombs in the courtiers' cemeteries that clustered around Old Kingdom pyramids.

The Egyptian pharaoh did not necessarily perform magic himself. Instead, he surrounded himself with trained magicians, like the pharaoh of the Exodus story. Tales written down on papyrus, and circulated for hundreds of years, recount the exploits of magicians with royal connections. One series of stories that was written down around 1600 BCE features King Khufu, builder of the Great Pyramid at Giza, who reigned a thousand years earlier. A bored Khufu challenges his sons to entertain him with tales of wonder. In the third of the five stories, Prince Baufre recalls how Khufu's father Snefru once had his chief reading-priest, Djadjaemankh, use magic to turn a wax boat into a real boat and fill it with twenty gorgeous young women, dressed only in strings (or perhaps fishnets) of shimmering faience beads. Snefru enjoyed the chance to have the women row him around a pleasure lake at the palace, until their boat abruptly stopped: one of the rowers had dropped a fish-shaped pendant into the water. Djadjemankh came to the rescue by stacking one half of the lake upside down onto the other, thus retrieving the pendant. It wasn't quite as dramatic as parting the Red Sea, perhaps, but it seems to have done the trick for old Snefru – and hearing about it cheered Khufu up, too.

When it's the turn of Prince Hardedef to entertain his father Khufu, he asks permission to bring a magician named Djedi to the royal court. Djedi is 110 years old, with the appetite of an ox, and such magical prowess that he can tame a lion and re-attach a man's severed head. Djedi also knows all about the secret chambers in the temple of the god Thoth, which Khufu would like to find so that he can have their magical inscriptions copied into his own temple. Djedi arrives and makes an excellent impression on Khufu and his court. The magician refuses to let Khufu chop off a prisoner's head just to see if he can reattach it. They settle for a goose instead. Djedi also demonstrates that he can make a lion walk peacefully behind him, without even using a leash, but when Khufu asks the old wise man about the secret chambers of Thoth, Djedi launches into another layered story that instead predicts the rise of a new dynasty of kings, who would be born as triplets to a woman named Redjedet. That wasn't quite the answer that Khufu was hoping for, but a recurring theme in Egyptian literature is that not even a pharaoh can know all the secrets of the cosmos. Only a magician could even begin to access the wisdom of Thoth, and only with great difficulty and at great personal risk.

The sorcerer-prince

In later periods of Egyptian history, a protagonist named Setne featured in tales that emphasized how badly things could go wrong for magicians who came too close to the sacred books in which Thoth had written down all the secrets of the universe. 'Setne' was not a personal name but a version of the *sem*-priest title as it was historically held by the high priests of the creator-god Ptah at Memphis, one of the largest cities in ancient Egypt, near modern-day Cairo. The tales were written down in Demotic during the Ptolemaic and Roman eras, but the high priest in question was one of the eldest sons of King Ramses II, Prince Khaemwaset, who lived around 1280 to 1200 BCE. Khaemwaset was one of many learned, influential priests

Opposite Prince Khaemwaset, son of Ramses II and priest of Ptah – the inspiration for the Setne stories.

throughout Egyptian history who were immortalized in literature and remembered as wise men and magicians. However, the Setne stories poke gentle fun at this sorcerer-prince, using him to convey moral lessons about the great responsibility that a great magician had.

In the earliest complete Setne tale, written on a papyrus now held in the British Museum, Setne discovers the tomb of a priest-magician named Naneferkaptah. The tomb is in the cemetery that served Memphis, called Saqqara, where we know the real Khaemwaset undertook restorations to old monuments as part of his priestly duties. In the story, Setne, like Khufu, is on the hunt for the secret book of Thoth, which he has heard is buried with Naneferkaptah.

Beginning of a Demotic papyrus scroll with the first Setne story.

As any ancient Egyptian should have known, trespassing on a tomb was the gravest of crimes, and sure enough, Setne finds himself face-to-face with the ghosts of Naneferkaptah, his wife Ikhweret, and their young son Merab. The ghost of Ikhweret begins to tell their tragic tale to Setne, both to warn him against the folly of seeking the Book of Thoth and to ask his help in reuniting this ghostly family, whose burials – as her story-within-a-story explains – are divided between Saqqara and the southern town of Koptos.

It transpires that Naneferkaptah was a prince and a sorcerer as well (in fact, the Setne tales hint that there were other stories, now lost, that featured the exploits of Naneferkaptah). One day, while Naneferkaptah was fulfilling his duties as a priest, reading from a scroll during a sacred procession, another priest offered to tell him the whereabouts of the Book of Thoth, in exchange for a bribe. Naneferkaptah can't resist, and having extracted the information from his colleague, he convinces Ikhweret to sail with him up the Nile to Koptos with their son. At Koptos, Naneferkaptah makes a boat and crew out of wax, recites a spell to animate them, and sets sail for the secret book's hidden location. When he reaches the point that his colleague described, Naneferkaptah casts sand into the water to divide it in two. He fights his way past the snake that guards the book, cutting it in half and putting sand between the severed pieces so that it cannot come back to life. Evil reptile defeated, Naneferkaptah works his way through the layered boxes that conceal the book: first iron, then bronze, wood, ebony and ivory, silver, and finally a box of pure gold with the papyrus scroll inside.

Eagerly, Naneferkaptah takes hold of the scroll and unrolls it, reading its spells and so gaining the ability to enchant all of nature. He sees a vision of the sun-god Ra shining in heaven and, at the same time, the rising of the moon and the stars. Magic, he understands, is what controls the cosmos, and Naneferkaptah, a magician and a prince, but nonetheless a mere human, now has power over it. He returns to his wife Ikhweret, hands her the book, and she – a princess and an educated woman – also reads the spells and has the same wondrous experience as her husband. Naneferkaptah uses fresh ink and papyrus to make a copy of the scroll, and soaks the copy in beer. He then dissolves the soggy scroll in water and drinks it, imbibing the magical texts into his own body. This consumption of magic words and images was a core component of Egyptian magical practice.

When Thoth discovers that Naneferkaptah has taken his secret book, he complains to Ra about the grave offence. This is the warning, and the plea, that Ikhweret presents to Setne: having knowledge that you should not possess is deadly. As she and her husband start their homeward journey downriver, their boat suddenly stops, and their beloved son Merab falls into the river and drowns. Not even Naneferkaptah can bring him back to life, so they return to Koptos to have the child embalmed and bury him there. Setting out a second time, in a more sombre mood, their boat is once again halted in the same spot. Ikhweret falls into the river and drowns, and her husband has to repeat the sorrowful return to Koptos, where he has her embalmed and buried with their son. The third time he prepares to sail forth from Koptos, Naneferkaptah takes a strip of royal linen, binds the Book of Thoth to his body, and waits for the inevitable to happen. When the boat stops, Naneferkaptah appears on deck and falls into the river, but his body can't be found. The boat sails on without him, and when it arrives at the docks in the Memphis, the king and court come to greet it, in mourning. Pharaoh spies Naneferkaptah, dead but magically holding fast to the boat's rudder, with the Book of Thoth still tied to his body. He orders a fine burial for Naneferkaptah in Saqqara, and has the deadly scroll hidden away within it.

Hearing all of this from the ghost of Ikhweret, Setne knows the danger that awaits him – but he ignores her warning. Setne manages to get the Book of Thoth away from Naneferkaptah and takes it to the pharaoh's court, where he reads the magic that it contains. As Ikhweret predicted, Setne is soon plagued with misfortune. He falls in lust with a beautiful priestess named Tabubu, who refuses to sleep with him unless he signs over all his worldly goods to her and disinherits his own children. Drunk on wine and sexual desire (a betrayal of his priestly responsibilities), Setne agrees. He falls into a deep sleep, and sees his children murdered and fed to dogs. When he wakes to find himself naked, shivering, and alone, he wonders what he has done.

Fortunately, it was all a dream – or a nightmare – and a chastened Setne returns the Book of Thoth to the tomb of Naneferkaptah. The tomb-owner's ghost thanks him and asks a favour, which Setne gladly undertakes, now that he is back on the priestly path. Setne sails to Koptos and searches its cemeteries for three days and three nights, until he finds the tomb where Ikhweret and Merab were buried all those centuries ago. He brings their mummies to Saqqara and buries them in the tomb with Naneferkaptah. It's as close to a happy ending as any magician could hope for.

These sets of stories reveal the status of magic in ancient Egypt: magicians were welcomed at the royal court and granted privileges, like the fine burial arranged for Naneferkaptah. They also help us understand what kind of people practised magic: Djadjemankh was a chief reading-priest, as from the sound of it was Naneferkaptah, while Khaemwaset was a *sem*-priest and good old Djedi seems to have had no title at all, but a reputation that reached the ears of a prince. Finally, they show us specific examples of magical techniques, such as the conjuration of a boat and its crew, and the sources of magical knowledge, such as the secret books and chambers of Thoth. These may be tales of wonder, which we would file under fiction today, but they were telling some magical truths.

Magic men and wise women

From princes to paupers, what most magicians in Egypt had in common was their membership of a priesthood. Magic was never really just entertainment for bored kings. It was linked to the supernatural world of the gods, and thus to the everyday world of the Egyptian temple. Temples were a crucial vehicle of the Egyptian state. They owned agricultural land and livestock, as well as running workshops for the production of all kinds of commodities, from works of art to food, textiles, and burial equipment. They organized religious festivals, kept archives and libraries, and helped monitor the Nile to gauge the all-important annual flood as it swelled the river from south to north each summer.

Egyptian temples ranged from vast complexes that dominated the surrounding landscape to more modest compounds in small villages. Regardless of their size, however, every temple needed priests. Most priests came from leading local families, and as there was no restriction on priests having wives and children, priestly positions tended to be handed down from father to son (as was the case with most occupations in ancient Egypt). Priests had to be able to read and write, so as children, they might already have attended temple-based schools.

Being a priest wasn't necessarily a full-time role. It could be combined with other responsibilities, such as owning and running an agricultural estate. Large temples divided the priesthood into four or five groups that worked in rotation, each looking after the temple rituals and other business for two or three months of the year. During that period, priests were meant to follow restrictions on what they ate and how they dressed, and may have lived in the temple to help maintain the required state of purity (which included observing sexual abstinence). In smaller temples, with a smaller population to draw on, these rules and rotas may have been more flexible. Nor should we imagine that when a priest wasn't officially on duty in the temple, he was completely off duty in his daily life. Once everyone knows that you have a level head, or a sympathetic ear, it's difficult to pass a petitioner on to whoever happens to be in charge at the temple that month. The same held true if your priestly path meant that you'd gained a reputation as an accomplished magician or talented healer.

Magic rituals and temple rites have many things in common, which means that almost every priest in some way came into contact

Sem-priest in a leopard-skin, with vases
of cleansing water and an incense burner.

with *heka* in the course of carrying out his temple duties. But only certain priests specialized in magic. This reflects the division of the priesthood into different types or categories. One category of priest closely associated with magic was the *sem*-priest, like Setne. The *sem* was a role that a priest or other individual of rank took on for certain ritual performances, and the *sem* is easily identifiable in art by the leopard skin draped across his body. *Sem*-priests officiated at a ritual called 'Opening the Mouth', which was performed to bring a living spirit into the body of a finished statue or an embalmed mummy.

The priest most closely associated with magic was the *khery-heb*, or reading-priest; some, like Djadjaemankh, attained the higher rank of chief reading-priest. Egyptologists usually term these men lector priests, from the Latin word for reading. In ancient Egyptian, *khery-heb* meant 'carrier of the scroll', and in visual representations of the reading-priest at work, he is often shown reciting from a scroll of papyrus that he unrolls between his hands. The *khery-heb* was someone especially learned and literate, who had full access to the libraries of texts that temples held. Perhaps the reading-priest also had a special gift for chanting these texts during rituals, since speaking the rites, as we've seen, was as important as being able to read them.

The *sem* and the *khery-heb* worked in the service of a whole range of gods and goddesses in temples all over Egypt. But there was one goddess whose priesthood had specific magical expertise: the *wab*-priests of the goddess Sekhmet specialized in healing. *Wab*, meaning 'pure' or 'clean', was a relatively lower rank of priest, but Sekhmet was a fitting focus for this type of magical specialism – this lion-headed goddess was believed to have power over illnesses that had no obvious physical cause. We now would identify many of these illnesses as infectious diseases caused by bacteria, viruses, or parasites, but in ancient Egypt, such afflictions seemed to strike from nowhere and, even worse, spread among families and communities. Supernatural causes were the natural explanation, and priests of Sekhmet were thus

best equipped to help with medical complaints – both in Egyptian mythological thought, and in our own terms of practical hygiene.

Another class of magicians with a specialization were scorpion-charmers, known as the *kherep* of Serket (or Selket), the goddess associated with scorpions. A *kherep* was a sceptre or wand, which as a hieroglyph symbolized having power over something. Hence the *kherep* of Serket was someone who had power over scorpions. These specialists are often found listed among the personnel of state-sponsored mining expeditions that had to face the dangers of travelling across deserts, home of scorpions and other deadly creatures.

There are two general terms for magical specialists that don't seem to link the practitioner to a specific deity or priesthood. One was *rekh-khet*, 'knower of rites', and the other simply *hekau*, the same expression – 'possessor of magic' – that had been used in the Old Kingdom to describe the king. By the Middle Kingdom (a few hundred years later), it seems to have become a more general term for a magician. A wooden statue representing a man named Djehutyhotep identifies him as 'leader of the *hekau*', as well as a scribe, and the bag that he holds in his right hand may be a container for some of the equipment he required in his line of magical work.

That equipment will have included amulets, either made by Djehutyhotep himself or by special amulet-makers called *sau*, after the word *sa*, meaning both 'amulet' and 'protection'. Like *hekau*, the term *sau* is used broadly. Some amulet-makers were probably magicians themselves. They may have been attached to temple workshops, where amulets in materials such as faience, glass, metals, and semi-precious stones were often made. At certain times in ancient Egyptian history, the circulation of these materials was restricted, especially where

Opposite Wooden statuette of Djehutyhotep,
leader of the *hekau* (magicians).

unusual technologies or rare materials were involved. Getting your hands on a carnelian *tyet*-amulet or a faience *wadjet*-eye required the right connections.

Producing faience, shaping glass, and casting bronze all required specialist knowledge and equipment, and making amulets out of these materials was a form of magic in itself. Invented as early as 3500 BCE, faience is a material the ancient Egyptians called *tjehenet*, from the word for 'shining' or 'luminous'. Similar to glazed pottery (but without the inclusion of clay), faience was made from a paste of ground quartz, which included silica particles, with plant ash, natron salt, and copper ore; when fired in a kiln, the silica and copper in this dull mixture fused into a glossy blue-green surface, which looks almost like a polished stone. Early glass technology, which developed much later, around 1600 BCE, required even more control of silica and minerals that provided colouring agents, while casting bronze and other metal alloys was its own skill, and one for which the ancient Egyptians were well-known in the ancient world. Today we would explain these transformations of raw materials by chemistry, but in antiquity they worked by, and like, magic.

Many amulets were made of much simpler materials, as we saw with the linen and papyrus amulets in the last chapter, which the magician could make on the spot for his client. The magical effect of amulets made of knotted cloth, or tiny folded packets of papyrus, lay in the words that were written on them, spoken over them, or both. Scorpion-charmer or amulet-maker, *khery-heb* or plain old *hekau*, there were clearly many ways to refer to magicians in ancient Egypt, not all of which map easily onto modern terms such as wizard, sorcerer, or healer. Nor, as you might have noticed, have we mentioned a witch or a sorceress, since what is missing here is approximately half the population: the women.

Though not well attested in ancient texts (which were written, for the most part, by and for men), women almost certainly had their own ways with magic in ancient Egypt. However, the female version of *hekau*, spelled *hekat*, is only ever used in a derogatory way, to describe a female magical practitioner who wasn't considered Egyptian; in that sense, it means something like witch, with a negative connotation. What does survive from ancient Egypt are a few references to female magical practitioners or wise women, using the word *rekhet*, 'she who knows', similar to the expression *rekh-khet* for a male magician. Letters written in the Old and Middle Kingdoms suggest that these wise women could contact the dead. We can also take it for granted that women helped other women give birth, since midwifery is such a common practice across human societies. As we'll see in Chapter 6, childbirth came with its own set of magic rites. Women were not full-fledged magicians, according to the hierarchy of the Egyptian temple, but they nonetheless performed magic of a different sort, when only a woman's touch would do.

Turned to stone

In the hierarchy of Egyptian priesthoods, magicians belonged to the temple's 'House of Life' (*per ankh*). The House of Life was both a place – a sort of library and learning centre – and a social institution, like a club or brotherhood to which magicians and other important priests belonged. Its influence lasted as long as the temples did, into the Late Roman period and beyond. The House of Life was an earthly version of the secret chambers of Thoth, full of wisdom and knowledge that could serve society beyond the temple walls. In the House of Life, it was the life of the community that was at stake: its heritage, its memories, and its health.

Priests who trained and served together in the House of Life formed close bonds. Close enough that in the 4th century BCE, the priests of the cat-goddess Bastet at a temple in the Delta clubbed together to erect a special statue in the form of a pious priest, in honour of three of their colleagues: Padimahes, Pasherimut, and Pasheribastet. These three men were not necessarily magicians, according to the titles they held, but they must have had some qualities that made them deserving of a statue, and in particular a statue like this one. For like similar statues known from other temples in Egypt, this statue played a special role in the life of the temple and its local community: it was a magical statue, used for healing and protection and, we think, available to anyone who came to the temple for help. It may originally have stood in a courtyard in front of the temple, perhaps in a small chapel of its own; the inner rooms of the temple itself were always off-limits to anyone other than the priests.

There are two clues to the statue's function: first, the inscriptions that cover almost every inch of its surface, and second, the object that the priest is holding between his hands. Carved from a form of sandstone known as greywacke, the statue is exquisitely made and highly finished. Its dark, polished surface is incised with magical images and hieroglyphic spells, from the cloth kerchief that covers the priest's head to the edge of the ankle-length garment he wears. The calm, noble-looking figure, with his left leg forward in the stance typical for statues of men, is probably a generic stand-in for all three of the priests that the statue honoured, who appear individually across the statue's abdomen, carved in recessed relief, in the act of praying to Bastet and her son Mahes, a lion-headed war god.

Between the hands of the statue is a stela, or cippus, showing a deity called Horus-on-the-crocodiles, for reasons that quickly become obvious. Hundreds of such objects survive, in every size, from wearable pendants, to amulets that would fit in a hand to sizeable standalone sculptures (see page 118). The central image on

Opposite Dark stone statue honouring three priests of
Bastet, with a healing stela of Horus-on-the-crocodiles.

58

the front shows the god Horus as a child, standing on the afore-mentioned crocodiles and grasping reptiles and wild animals in his hands. The scene represents his magical mastery over dangerous forces, and many of the magic spells written over the statue's surface use stories of Isis and young Horus to repel the effects of snake bites and scorpion stings. Other spells, together with the emblems carved alongside them, have a more general protective function. They tie the statue and the Horus image into the astral powers of the cosmos and creation.

Statues like this one, or a Horus stela on its own, worked by using sacred water to absorb magic words and images – which were, after all, the same thing, given the pictorial character of hieroglyphic writing. Just as, in the Setne story, the magician Naneferkaptah dissolved a copy of the Book of Thoth first in beer and then water and drank it, the water poured over the surface of a magical statue or stela would absorb the power of the hieroglyphs. Cups or basins placed below would catch the energized water, which took on healing properties. Or at least, that's what visitors to these statues must have hoped.

Not coincidentally, perhaps, the water running over the front of this statue also covered the personal names and incised images of Padimahes and his fellow priests. We can tell by their names that the three men were all local boys: Padimahes means 'The child given by Mahes', while Pasheribastet is 'The child of Bastet' and Pasherimut is 'The child of Mut', another goddess worshipped nearby. So it may be that in helping to bless the water to help local people, the statue was also helping to bless these men, as well as commemorate their memory for as long as the statue stood. Adventure stories weren't the only way that the reputations of wise priests, gifted healers, and talented magicians were preserved. Through statues, monuments, and their family tombs, priests and magicians became part of the Egyptian landscape, their names, feats, and memories passed down through generations.

But how did men like Padimahes and his colleagues become priests – and potentially magicians – in the first place? The ability to read and write was essential, so training in magic began, for boys, in the scribal schools situated in temples throughout Egypt. The rare women who acquired this skill probably did so at home, from male relatives. But being able to read and write wasn't enough to get you into the priesthood, much less make a magician out of you; as we have seen, priestly roles often ran in families, and having connections may have been as much, if not more, important than natural ability when it came to joining a certain priesthood. Lineage mattered in ancient Egypt.

Many of the things a magical expert needed to know could probably only be learned through in-person observation, and one-on-one apprenticeships would surely have served to protect the secrecy that so many rites required. Finding and using magic materials, learning the correct gestures to use, and hearing the right words, spoken in the right way, were things a would-be magician could only learn from a master. And the magic spells collected in the Pyramid Texts, the later Coffin Texts, and the Book of the Dead (which the Egyptians called the 'Book of Going Forth by Day') may give us a glimpse into some of the tests that priests and magicians had to pass to demonstrate their proficiency once their training had been completed. Some form of initiation, known as 'seeing the horizon', seems to have marked a priest's formal entrance into service, once a trainee had acquired sufficient knowledge to perform rites safely and could be trusted by his fellow priests to fulfil his duties independently.

The judgment ceremony in the Book of the Dead, known by scholars as spell (or chapter) 125, may be based on just such an initiation rite. In this scene, the heart of the deceased is weighed against the feather of truth (*maat*), so that they can join Osiris in the underworld, as long as they are judged worthy; they then became known in ancient Egyptian as 'true of voice', often translated as 'justified'.

The judgment scene from the *Book of the Dead*
made for Ani and his wife Tutu.

In the judgment spell, the deceased – perhaps originally, the priestly initiate – declares his (sometimes her) purity, honour, and virtue, the same qualities that Setne temporarily abandoned in his lust for Tabubu. Other bad behaviour that had to be denied included eating unclean foods, having illicit sex, fiddling your account books, and stealing from the temple's cattle herds.

Like the judgment scene, many other spells in the Book of the Dead seem to originate from the secret knowledge kept in the House of Life. In the context of a burial, where they were written on papyrus or painted on coffins and tomb walls, such scenes and spells take on a double layer of meaning. Spells for becoming a bird, having power over the elements, and joining the boat of the sun-god express the dead person's hope of an empowered life in the next world – that ability to 'come forth by day' from the darkness of the tomb. But they also reflect the kinds of ritual knowledge that only priests could possess, and some of the powers that magicians could wield. Over time, these powers included fantastic abilities such as flying (if you're a bird, you're halfway there) or becoming invisible, as was the purpose of this tantalizing spell from Roman times:

> Take a falcon's egg. Gild half of it and coat the other half
> with cinnabar [red mercuric sulfide]. While wearing this,
> you will be invisible when you say the name.

Unfortunately, the writer has neglected to indicate what exactly that name would be, although we're assured that the spell is both 'marvellous' and 'practical'. No wonder ancient texts sometimes baffle our uninitiated ears and eyes.

But knowledge was power. An experienced priest-magician will have internalized an astonishing array of information as part of his training, from the manifold names of deities, demi-gods, and demons, to the plants and minerals that were the core ingredients in healing concoctions and protective potions. In the judgment of the dead, give the wrong answer and your cheating heart would be eaten by the monster Ammut, condemning you to a state of powerless non-being. For magicians passing from their training days to full-fledged practice, just as much was at stake for themselves, their clients, and the entire cosmos. The natural and the supernatural worlds were intertwined, like the world of the living and the world of the dead – and a magician needed to know how to handle both.

3

DEALING WITH THE DEAD

Even as legendary a magician as Setne balked at a trip to the under-world. It was one thing rummaging around tombs and talking to ghosts – that was all in a day's work. But venturing into the actual realm of the dead was another thing entirely. What happened after death had to remain a mystery, even to a sorcerer-prince. Or did it?

In another of the Setne tales, we find our hero relaxing at home when he sees two funeral processions pass by. The first is clearly for a rich man: a train of priests and mourners accompany a beautifully bedecked coffin towards a fine tomb, where the choicest meat, best beer, and finest linen will be left as offerings to his spirit, together with alabaster vessels of the purest perfume oils. Behind this luxuri-ous procession, Setne spies another: a rough-woven mat encases the body of a poor man, being carried alone to a humble grave. Angered, Setne rails against the injustice of life and death. Why should the rich enjoy a blessed afterlife, while the poor, who had no access to mummification rites or funds for an elaborate burial and funerary offerings, were deprived of any kind of eternal existence? Setne's precocious son, Sa-Osiris, suggests that they go to the underworld to see for themselves – a journey so dangerous that it can only be done with the help of Sa-Osiris's own magical powers. Sometimes it helps to have a wizard for a child.

Lo and behold, the afterlife has served up just desserts. The rich man with the flashy funeral has been condemned; Setne and his son witness him wailing in eternal pain because his eye socket has been used as the pivot on which one of the many gates to the underworld swings open and shut. It's the poor man, laid in an unmarked grave, who stands shining and dressed in pure white cloth, having passed successfully through the judgment and joined the gods. Both men's actions, behaviour, and character during their lifetimes determined their fates after death. All the expense and effort that went into building and decorating a tomb, filling it with luxurious goods, and having your corpse embalmed, wrapped, and sealed in an elaborate coffin (or three): these were all for nothing, if you hadn't lived honourably in your time on earth.

If equipping a tomb wasn't enough to secure eternal life, why did so many ancient Egyptians keep doing it? One reason, of course, is that it's always the living who bury the dead. That means we have to look to Egyptian society at large to understand practices like mummification, funeral rites, and tomb decoration. These practices reflect much wider beliefs about the supernatural, not only those of the deceased. Such beliefs were central to how the Egyptians made sense of the natural world and its cycles of birth, death, and renewal. The afterlife had its secrets, to be sure, but secrets were a magician's speciality. Dealing with the dead was a lot easier with expert help, as we'll see on our own tour through the underworld.

The shadow land

The underworld, the netherworld, the afterlife, the great beyond, heaven and hell: there are so many ways to refer to what we can only imagine – what happens to us when we are no longer alive. In ancient Egyptian, the dead occupy an otherworld called the Duat. In some ways, the Duat resembled the natural world that the Egyptians knew. But in other, quite important, ways, it was an alternate reality, where bizarre creatures and strange spirits that defied the laws of logic lurked.

For a place that could only be imagined, not experienced, the Duat had some surprisingly specific features. Maps, images, and texts detail its landscape of caverns, deserts, dangerous rivers, and fiery lakes, each with its own terrible name. The Duat was a land of shadow and darkness. It was ice cold, or blazing hot. The ground could tremble and shake, and booming noises split the silence. Obstacles, traps, and tortuous paths made it difficult to get your bearings. Yet the Duat had an eerie familiarity as well. It was a mirror-image of the land of the living. A warped mirror, to be sure, but like the natural and the supernatural, this world and the next could not exist without each other.

The Duat was often imagined as being located somewhere in the west, the land of the setting sun and therefore associated with the dead. Yet the Duat was not contained within a single cardinal point. It encompassed the entire cosmic landscape through which the sun-god Ra had to travel overnight in order to be reborn in the east at dawn. This journey through the Duat and the twelve hours of the night was the theme of many of the so-called 'Underworld Books' found on the walls of royal tombs in the New Kingdom, parts of which were also copied onto other objects. These compositions contain such complex images and complicated hieroglyphic inscriptions that Egyptologists are still working to make sense of some of them today.

Like all gods, Ra travelled in a boat, surrounded by an entourage of gods and demi-gods to help navigate, sail the boat, and protect him. In the Duat, Ra faced the ferocious serpent Apep, the embodiment of chaos and disorder, whose movements could make the earth tremble. Defeating Apep is at the core of many magic spells, which often identify the magician with the gods from which he draws his power, in opposition to the evil forces that Apep represents. The regeneration of Ra happened in the middle of the night, when the sun-god's boat passed through the secret canyon where Osiris was buried. It was the mystic union of the two gods that restored Ra's strength as dawn approached, resetting the cosmic cycle of renewal for another day.

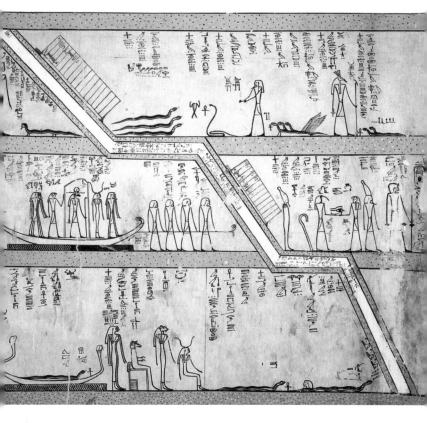

In the middle row of this scene on the walls of the tomb of
King Thutmose III in the Valley of the Kings, the sun-god Ra, standing
in his solar boat, faces the gates of the Duat.

To aid in their own regeneration, the dead were equipped with amulets and spells to help them find their way through the Duat, which was a risky place for anyone who wasn't already dead or divine. There were plenty of other Duat-dwelling demons who were named in magic spells, classed variously as enemies, adversaries, and the unjustified dead. These malevolent forces reversed all normal behaviour, feasting on excrement and facing backwards as they moved, with their body parts in all the wrong places. They were creatures who should be avoided if possible, or, failing that, kept at bay through the powers of magic.

What Setne saw in the Duat complicates any assumption that the ancient Egyptians believed you could buy your way into a blessed state. An eternal existence awaited you, but if you weren't properly prepared, it could be one that you, or your surviving relatives, might live to regret.

Spirit trouble

The dead were supposed to be in the Duat, whether judged 'true of voice' or otherwise. Trouble was, some of them lingered in the land of the living long after they died. They reappeared unexpectedly, anxious to protect their tombs, or looking to offer an unsolicited opinion from beyond the grave. All this to-ing and fro-ing from the underworld was a hazardous side-effect of the wishes expressed in collections of funeral magic like the Coffin Texts and the Book of the Dead, or the Book of Going Forth by Day. The blessed dead wanted to be able to move freely between the Duat and the world they'd left behind – which might present problems for those who still lived in it.

The spirits of the dead might have gone to the underworld, but their mortal remains were fairly close to hand. Cemeteries lined the desert edges of the Nile valley, their tombs often in plain view from village houses. Even in the fertile Delta, where agricultural land was at a premium, there was always room for a cemetery, usually located just outside a town. At some settlements, such as Gurob in the Fayum Oasis, newborns were buried at home, placed under the floor of a house they never knew, while at the village of Deir el-Medina, near the Valley of the Kings, there was a dedicated burial ground for infants and very young children. The very poor – like the man Setne saw, wrapped in a simple reed mat – might have had no proper burial at all, or at least not a burial that has left any trace for archaeologists to find.

While cemeteries were kept separate from residential areas, they were close enough to reach on special feast days, when families went to picnic and pray among the tombs of their ancestors. Those who could afford it paid cemetery priests to make regular offerings and recite prayers before the dead all year round; saying the name of the dead person in these prayers was especially important, given the strong link between a person's name and his or her identity. And of course there was nothing to prevent anyone from visiting an ancestor, family member, or friend, at any time. In fact, it was encouraged, and graffiti left inside the painted upper chapels of some New Kingdom tombs record visitors admiring the artists' work and honouring the tomb owner's memory.

For the most part, ancestral spirits were a force for good and a source of pride. Family lineage and reputation were vital to ancient Egyptians' sense of social identity. The good spirits of the dead were known as *akhu*, the 'shining' or 'illuminated' ones. Becoming an *akh* was the ultimate goal of the funerary rituals carried out for the dead, but as the story of Setne and Sa-Osiris suggests, to be among the blessed dead, a person should also have demonstrated a kind and generous character in life. To honour their ancestors, the Egyptians kept memorial shrines in their homes. A particular kind of sculpture, showing just the head and linen-wrapped shoulders of the deceased, was sometimes set up in these shrines to commemorate a particularly revered ancestor. Its form resembled the hieroglyph used to write the words 'god' or 'mummy', which would be appropriate for the otherworldly, semi-divine *akh* it was meant to represent. Through the magic of offerings left for the bust and the prayers recited in its presence, it was hoped that the *akh* would bless the home and family and keep them safe from harm.

Even good ghosts like the *akhu* could be a cause for concern. They were ghosts, after all, so their behaviour was unpredictable by nature. But still worse were the spirits known as *mwtw* (rhymes with 'tutu'). This was a generic term for the spirits of the dead, but one often used with a negative connotation – the *mwtw* were ghosts with ill intentions. They were blamed for many illnesses, mental anguish, and nightmares. Surviving spells show the kind of magical intervention required to banish the *mwtw* and other malevolent spirits:

> Oh male adversary or female adversary, male *akh* or female *akh*, be far away from So-and-so! Oh male *mwt* or female *mwt*, you will not come!

The magician went on to tell these evil forces that his client has already taken out their hearts and offered them up to 'The Striker', a rearing cobra who hissed protective fire from her mouth. Now known by the Latin word *uraeus*, from the Greek *ouraios* ('tail-standing'), itself derived the ancient Egyptian *iaret*, this was the cobra who sat on the foreheads of kings and deities. But it seems that the awe-inspiring uraeus could protect ordinary Egyptians, too. At the end of the spell, instructions in red ink told the magician to recite the text over four clay cobra figures 'with flames in their mouths', placing one in each corner of the room where people slept. Perhaps the clay cobras served a double purpose as night-lights, with a wick lit in oil to banish the deepest darkness.

What made the *mwtw*, in particular, so hostile to humans? Some *mwtw* may have been the ghosts of people who died violent or untimely deaths, and in later eras of Egyptian history, spells were sometimes placed in the tombs of such victims to guard against this. Perhaps they were those who had not been judged 'true of voice' and blessed with an eternity of peace. But any spirit could turn nasty, even a dear departed relative whose burial you had seen to yourself and whose offerings you had topped up, faithfully, for years. Well, more or less.

When troubles started to plague an Egyptian household, a niggling doubt could creep in. What if the ghost of a parent, a sibling, or perhaps your first wife, was causing all the trouble? The solution was to write the dead person a letter, or more likely, get the local scribe to compose it for you. Better yet, have the scribe write it on a pottery bowl or vase that you could fill with offerings of food and drink and leave in the tomb chapel. Such letters could also be written on sheets of papyrus, potsherds, or stelae. In one, a widower worried that his deceased wife was making him ill, though he asks about her own comforts first:

A communication by Merertifi to Nebitef. How are you?
Is the West taking care of you as you wish? Now, since I am
your beloved on earth, fight on my behalf and intercede
on behalf of my name. I did not garble a spell in your
presence, when I was perpetuating your name on earth.
Remove the infirmity from my body! Please become an
akh-spirit for me so that I may see you before my eyes, in
a dream, fighting on my behalf. I will then deposit offerings
for you at dawn and equip your offering table for you.

Some writers were even more blunt with their dead relatives. One son demanded that his dead parents seize hold of and stop whatever *mwt* was troubling him: 'The two of you are there [in the Duat], only looking after your own interests,' he wrote, chastising them for not looking after their offspring on earth. Another husband could have exercised greater tact in a long diatribe to his dead wife: 'I didn't divorce you when I became successful' perhaps isn't the most persuasive argument to use against a woman you believe to be ruining your life from the beyond. Nor, I suspect, were there special Duat points for not sleeping with the housemaids, as the same man added in his defence. Personally, I hope the spectral recipient of this letter, an *akh* named Ankhiry, ignored her husband's pleas for a while longer.

Even from the Duat, the dead maintained relationships with the world of the living – whether the living wanted them to or not. There were blessed dead, vengeful dead, and dead who could turn one way or the other, depending on what ailed them (or you). Becoming an *akh*-spirit – the good kind of ghost – was the ostensible goal of mummification and a good burial, but it seems that becoming such a luminous soul wasn't a one-step, one-off process. Like many forms of ritual, it required regular renewal so that the effects of the transformation didn't wear off, and regular offerings to honour the ancestors and stay on their good side. Magicians were called in to help control the spirits of the dead in part because magicians had the tools to protect themselves from any evil spirits with ill intentions, but there was another reason that magic was an apt response to troubled spirits from beyond: magic had helped them get there in the first place.

Magical mummies

Mummies are the most famous example of ancient Egyptian magic. But they are also the most poorly understood, thanks to fanciful Victorian fiction and Hollywood hype. The so-called 'curse of the mummy' twisted ancient magic into horror stories about Egyptian mummies that come back to life to seduce or, more often, take revenge on hapless archaeologists. But these stories are more revealing of the anxiety Western audiences felt about meddling with ancient graves and interfering with modern Egyptian sovereignty, after the colonial and imperial endeavours of the 19th and early 20th centuries, than the ancient Egyptians' rationale for mummification. In any case, if a mummy ever did feel like going on a rampage, some Egyptologists surely have had it coming to them.

Mummies are misunderstood for another reason, too. Egyptologists have long assumed that the goal of mummification was to preserve the body in as lifelike a way as possible, so that the dead person's spirit form (or forms) could recognize which body to return to in the tomb – which often got crowded, since tombs held entire families and might be reused over long periods of time. One problem with this explanation is that nobody but the embalming-priests ever saw the preserved corpse, and even they couldn't be sure it would stay in that state forever. Many mummified bodies are little more than skeletons. Preservation of muscle tissue, skin, and hair depends on the exact embalming process used, which varied greatly over time and in different places.

Moreover, once the corpse itself was embalmed, by whatever means, it was wrapped in hundreds of metres of linen bandages and shrouds (often including the deceased person's clothing), placed in at least one coffin (and up to three or four), sometimes covered again with a shroud, and finally sealed away in the farthest reaches of a tomb, or at the very least a nice big hole cut deep into the ground. Coffins tended to show the deceased transformed into gods, rather than their earthly selves, but inscriptions gave the dead person's name. The average spirit should have had no trouble recognizing its mummy and finding a safe place to rest among all the layers of coffins and wrappings.

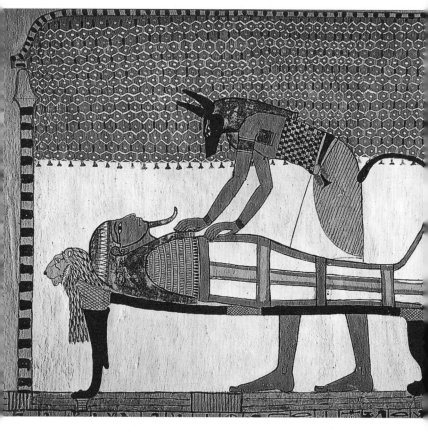

Anubis attends to a wrapped mummy under the embalming tent,
in the tomb of the artist Sennedjem at Deir el-Medina.

Mummification makes more sense if we think of it as a religious ritual – and if we remember that religious rituals were intricately connected to magic rites and Egyptian mythology. Washing the body was the first stage in caring for the dead, a practice common in many cultures, and on around the fifth day after death the family delivered the corpse to the embalming-priests, who did their work in a structure called the 'pure place', or *wabet*. In some cases, especially from the New Kingdom onwards, the embalming-priests removed the inner organs to stave off decay. The best quality mummifications involved doing this through a slit in the left side of the body, which was the 'unlucky' side of the body – and the most awkward side, anatomically, from which to work unless the embalmer used his left, equally unlucky, hand to reach into the abdominal cavity. The Greek visitor Diodorus wrote about this process after spending time in Egypt in the 1st century CE. According to his account, the poor priest who cut into the abdomen was chased out of the embalming tent afterwards, as if he had become tainted by doing the deed. The cut was made with a flake of obsidian sharpened to a knife edge, and an obsidian amulet that perhaps represented the fingers of the embalming-priest was often placed over the wound in the first layers of the mummy wrappings. The Egyptians would not have known that obsidian derived from the lava of ancient volcanic eruptions, but they nonetheless considered it a material with magical potential, thanks to its rarity (it was sourced from Ethiopia) and its strangely shiny, dark character.

What happened next in the embalmers' workshop involved the same materials that were used to purify the air in temple sanctuaries and anoint the statues of the gods who lived there, namely the burning of incense, cleansing with natron salt, and anointing with oil that was perfumed with precious resin. Incense kept the air sweet-smelling, while natron was a common detergent and bleaching agent in ancient Egypt. It also worked as a desiccant. There are different theories about

Amulet in the form of two fingers,
to protect the embalming incision.

how it worked in embalming (and there were probably different ways of using it, in any case), but if the embalming-priests packed the corpse with natron and left it for some time, the salt drew moisture out of the body, further arresting the process of decay. Soaking the body in a natron solution is another possible method, as if the embalmers were brining or pickling the dead. In fact, Greek writers called the Egyptian embalming-priests 'the picklers'.

Next came the application of oils, the 'balsams' from which our word 'embalming' derives. The sweet-smelling resin of myrrh trees was heated with plant oils to create a rich, perfumed substance. Not only was the oil applied to the skin of the body, but it was also layered with linen bandages as the wrapping part of the mummification process began. Some mummies were so thickly impregnated with resinous oils that when they were unwrapped in the 19th and early 20th centuries (when unwrapping was standard practice), the procedure became more of a chiselling, to break through the hardened substance. The mummy of Tutankhamun, for instance, was stuck fast in its innermost, solid gold coffin from the resinous oil that had been poured over it, and the famous gold mummy mask was stuck over the wrapped face of the young pharaoh. Excavator Howard Carter and his colleagues heated up knives to soften the ancient resin and prise the mask off the head, after detaching it from the king's body.

The total length of time a proper mummification took was seventy days, a number that corresponded to the time it took for certain constellations – the decans, from the Greek word for 'ten' – to travel across the sky from the eastern horizon to the west. A new decan appeared in the east every ten days, just before dawn. Egyptian astronomers identified each of these constellations with a god or goddess and related them to ideas about the night sky, the Duat, and rebirth. The decans could be represented inside the lids of coffins or on the ceilings of tombs, emphasizing the connection between the dead person's mummification and hoped-for rebirth and the cyclical renewal of the universe itself. Embalming the corpse took up to forty days from the day the person had died, leaving a good thirty days in this seventy-day ritual for the important stage of wrapping the body in all those bandages and shrouds.

Mummification obviously involved some pretty big ideas, including some magical ones. While the embalming and especially the wrapping processes were being carried out, a reading-priest (the *kheryheb*) was on hand to recite the necessary ritual formulas. Word and action went together, as in any magic rite, and the circular action of wrapping the body – finger by finger, limb by limb – helped embed protection and wholeness right into it. Placing amulets over the body at different stages of the wrapping was another magical procedure. In the Late Period (*c.* 650 to 350 BCE), some mummies had hundreds of amulets secreted among their wrappings, both on the body and in between the layers of linen. Obviously, the fact that we know about these amulets means that their protective power had its limits.

Front of a funerary amulet for Hatnefer
in the shape of a scarab, a common protective symbol.

Ancient tomb robbers were not averse to attacking mummies in search of precious stones and metals, while in more recent times, anatomists and archaeologists unwrapped mummies with such enthusiasm that the amulets are sometimes all that survives.

The types of amulets that were placed within the mummy wrappings changed over time, but common examples included the red carnelian *tyet* knot, the *djed* pillar (often in blue-green faience), and a scarab placed on the chest, inscribed with a spell imploring it not to testify against the deceased at the judgment. Amulets representing

Back of Hatnefer's amulet, inscribed with a spell
compelling her heart to speak well of her at the judgment.

the Four Sons of Horus were often placed over the abdomen. Each of
these minor gods was associated with a different part of the viscera
that were removed in the most thorough form of embalming: stomach,
lungs, liver, and intestines. The Four Sons were also painted on the
midsection of coffins and, in many elite burials, took the form of jars
in which the mummified organs were stored. Sometimes all of the
Four Sons had human heads, but often they had a range of human
and animal heads, in keeping with Egyptian conventions for representing otherworldly beings. Imsety, protector of the liver, always had

Painted wooden stela that shows Tabimut, at right, praying
to several divinities, including the Four Sons of Horus at left.

a human head; Duamutef, for the stomach, had a jackal head; Hapi, for the lungs, had the head of a baboon; and Qebehsenuef, for the intestines, had a falcon's head, taking after their father.

The power of magic went beyond caring for the corpse itself. Magical methods were also employed to help the deceased find peace in the Duat. For the spirit to live contentedly, as we've seen, regular prayers and offerings were required. However, a degree of magical insurance could be built into the burial. Paintings of banquets or bountiful harvests on tomb walls, stelae inscribed with prayers that promised offerings to the spirit, or models that showed the production of food, beer, and cloth, could all help make perpetual funerary offerings a magical reality. Representing ideal offerings in words and images meant that they could be activated, by magic, to help keep the tomb's spirits well-nourished and well-disposed.

While an elaborate burial was no guarantee of a happy eternal existence, as Sa-Osiris and his father Setne saw during their visit to the underworld, the most privileged members of ancient Egyptian society clearly commissioned a barrage of magical techniques in hopes of securing an optimal afterlife. Mummification was a privilege and a sacred rite, and even if it became more common over time, the poorest and most marginalized of people will not have had anything like the kinds of burials that make news headlines or fill entire museum galleries. Magic shows us clearly that Egypt in ancient times was neither a happy-go-lucky place, nor a society of equals. For some, death will have come as a relief, whatever lay beyond.

Faience hippopotamus with lotus flowers on its body.
Three of its legs were broken off in antiquity.

A MAGICAL MENAGERIE

Hunting a hippopotamus is not an activity that is recommended, not only for ethical and legal concerns, but also for practical reasons. They are extraordinarily large creatures, for a start, and aggressive when it comes to defending their young from predators or other hippopotami. The jaw of a hippopotamus can clamp shut in seconds, and although hippopotamus teeth are designed for a plant-based diet, they also have long, curved incisors that grow to a point. An aggrieved hippo can easily run down a human, or overturn a boat. So please, no hippo-hunting in real life – but a little hippo could come in handy for your ventures in magic.

A hippo as little as the span of your hand, to be precise. Archaeologists have found shiny blue figures of hippopotami in a range of postures in Middle Kingdom and slightly later burials. These hippos all have two things in common. First, they are primarily made of faience, the glazed paste so tricky to produce that it was believed to have mysterious, magical qualities. These hippos were made from a closely guarded recipe, pressed into moulds and fired in a kiln to bring forth their blue shimmer. Often, a black, manganese-based glaze decoration was painted on before a piece went into the kiln; the hippos' bodies are adorned with lotus leaves, buds, and blossoms, making it seem as though the animal has merged with the plants that grew in the riverine marshes that were its home.

As if that weren't magical enough, these hippo figures have a second thing in common: each had a foot broken off or damaged when it was placed in the tomb. Some may even have been broken in two. This doesn't fit our modern idea of how such beautifully made objects should look, and many museums or private collectors have replaced the missing foot to make the hippo appear intact. In ancient Egypt, however, these figures weren't made to be looked at and admired. They were made to be used. The breakage is all that remains of the magic ritual that was their entire reason for being. Reduced to manageable size, and in their magic-imbued faience form, these hippopotami helped the priest-magician in charge of the burial control the destructive power of the animal and all it symbolized. Once the figure had been hobbled and tamed by magic words and actions, it may also have served the double purpose of protecting the tomb and the dead from harm. Not a decorative object, then, which is what these striking blue hippos have become in museum gift shops. At the Metropolitan Museum of Art in New York, you can buy hippo-patterned socks in honour of their famous figurine, known as William. At least you get to keep both of your feet.

We've already seen that ancient Egyptian ideas about the supernatural world allowed for ghosts and spirits that could move between this world and the next, and that the gods and goddesses they worshipped could take human as well as animal form, or some mixture of the two. The god Osiris always took human form, reflecting his role as a mythical king, while his brother Seth, his son Horus, and his sister-wife Isis all appear in different human and animal forms. So does the sun-god Ra (usually with a falcon's head), who was accompanied on his daily journey across the sky and through the Duat by dozens of gods and demi-gods, each as weird and wonderful as the next. 'Demi-god' and 'minor god' serve as catch-all terms for supernatural beings that were not important enough to have huge temples built in their honour, but nonetheless played a key role in the world of the gods – and, therefore, in the world of magic and magicians.

This chapter looks at a panoply – a menagerie, even – of supernatural beings and their counterparts in the natural world. Human figures of different ages, genders, and body shapes were gleefully combined with parts of animals, birds, and reptiles of every imaginable variety. This wasn't because ancient Egyptians worshipped 'monsters', as the Roman satirist Juvenal rather harshly put it. Instead, this bewildering diversity of humans, animals, and creatures in-between enabled Egyptian artists – and magicians – to harness the potential of an otherwise invisible world. But with so many deities and demi-gods to choose from, how did a magician know which creature to conjure, and which to avoid? The physical forms that gods take in art and magical objects can help us understand some of the connections between them, as well as giving us an important insight into the purpose of images in magical practices. Like the hippopotamus figures that had to have a foot knocked off, any image made to represent a powerful animal, a semi-divine spirit, or a full-blown god had the potential to channel the supernatural energy of what it represented, and its potential dangers thus constrained.

Seeing the supernatural

The ancient Egyptians believed that the supernatural was everywhere – and nowhere, since it could not be perceived by normal senses like vision. Instead, supernatural forces made themselves known through unusual natural phenomena, like thunderstorms; through dream-like visions that some humans received; or through the heightened perceptions that magicians acquired during a rite.

The Egyptian gods that are most familiar to us – Osiris, Isis, and their son Horus; Thoth, the god of writing and wisdom; Amun, the creator-god of ancient Thebes; the sun-god Ra and his daughters, Sekhmet, goddess of war and disease, and Hathor, goddess of love and beauty – make up only one part of the divine world of ancient Egypt. Many of these deities can be traced to very early written sources, like the Pyramid Texts, and all of them qualify as a *netjer*, the Egyptian word for a major god or goddess. These major deities had complex mythologies and were worshipped all over Egypt, although they often had a specific centre of worship that may reveal their local roots, such as Dendera for Hathor, Abydos for Osiris, or Heliopolis (now part of Cairo) for Ra.

In the visual arts, the major deities developed standard characteristics that make them easy to recognize once you know what to look for. Some take the shape of attractive humans, distinguished by the crowns or hieroglyphic symbols on their heads: Isis and Hathor balance the hieroglyphic writings of their names on top of their beautiful dark hair, while Amun sports a crown made of two tall feathers. Others have the head of an animal poised atop the shoulders of a human body: a falcon for Horus and Ra, a lioness for Sekhmet, and an ibis for Thoth. But gods and goddesses could change their forms, too, and be represented by an animal alone: Hathor as a cow, Thoth as a baboon or an ibis, and Isis as the kite, a common bird of prey. We shouldn't assume that the ancient Egyptians imagined that their gods looked precisely like these figures. Instead, the beautiful bodies, human-animal composites, and animal avatars were ways to represent in physical form what only existed beyond the immediate physical limits of human experience.

In addition to all these major gods, the supernatural world was populated by myriad beings that could also take an even more astonishing, even bizarre, array of forms. This was in keeping with the way such beings functioned as adjuncts, or at times enemies, of the gods and as intermediaries between humans and the divine realm. Egyptologists have used several words to characterize these minor gods, since there is no single word in ancient Egyptian to categorize or describe them. The word 'minor' makes them sound unimportant, but they weren't, especially in Egyptian magic. To take just two examples, the dwarf-bodied god Bes and the hippo-hybrid goddess Taweret

Amulet depicting Horus as a young child, between
his mother Isis (left) and her sister Nephthys (right).

were both gods associated with the protection of households, women, and children, and appear in many magic images and spells as a result (both are discussed in more detail in Chapter 6). Some of the less familiar gods called on in magic spells were of non-Egyptian origin, like the goddesses Astarte and Qudshu from ancient Babylonia, or the Canaanite god Samanu, who was called upon in New Kingdom spells to cure skin disorders and other physical complaints. Their foreign, exotic quality was part of these deities' appeal, since magicians knew magic worked best the more mysterious it sounded.

Then there are the supernatural creatures that Egyptologists have variously referred to as demons or genies, or more generally as spirits, other than the *mwtw* and *akhu* whom we met in the last chapter. Demon – from the ancient Greek *daemon*, meaning a lesser deity – has come to have a negative connotation in English, and is often used to describe the harmful spirits encountered in magical texts. A demon was any force that might cause something bad to happen to you, and the purpose of many magic spells and amulets was to protect you from these manifestations of the great unknown. Such dangerous creatures were associated with ponds, canals, and wells, perhaps reflecting a fear of falling into deep water, or the unpleasant smell of standing water. Unnamed groups of demons also appear in magic spells, where they might be likened to the enemies who attack the sun-god in his solar boat. Some demons were messengers from the goddess Sekhmet, who brought disease, warfare, and strife into the world.

People in ancient Egypt reckoned time like we do, by the changing seasons and days of the month. There were three seasons in a year, each lasting four months: *Akhet*, when the Nile flood progressed from south to north (roughly July to October); *Peret*, when the flood receded and farmers could plant crops (November to February); and *Shemu*, the harvest (March to June). Each month had thirty days, with five extra days added between the end of *Shemu* and the beginning of *Akhet*, when the world waited for the unpredictable flood season to start and the new year to begin. These were days of celebration but also of danger, as demons ran amok. Egyptologists refer to these as the intercalary or epagomenal days, because they fall between the last and first calendrical months. Let's call them demon days, because they required special protection against Sekhmet's sinister henchmen. Magicians made special amulets out of linen or papyrus for people to wear during those trying times, surviving examples of which correspond to the spells and instructions known from magical handbooks. To make the demon-day amulets, the magician drew a series of gods in a row while reciting the spell, and the client wore it around his or her neck by means of twisted cords at either end. Some amulets have twelve figures drawn on them, corresponding to the twelve demons that Sekhmet was said to unleash, while others have five, clearly identifiable as Osiris, Isis, Seth, their sister Nephthys, and Horus. Each of these gods was said to have been born on one of the five demon days. Risky times brought some hope with them as well.

Papyrus amulet to be rolled up and worn during the 'demon days' at the end of the year.

Fantastic beasts

Demons, demi-gods, major gods: whatever we call them and however we categorize them, there's no question that animals both real and imagined were a vital part of magical practice in ancient Egypt. In fact, images of animals offer some of the earliest clues to the super-natural world of the Egyptians, long before the standard depictions of divinities emerged in visual imagery and hieroglyphic writing. On an intricately carved stone palette dating to the Predynastic era (*c.* 3200 BCE), a pair of lion-like animals with long, snake-like necks protectively surrounds a circular depression on one side of the object. Palettes like this are oversized versions of smaller, handheld palettes, where such depressions were used to grind the pigment painted onto participants in a ritual – perhaps a priest-magician, a ruler, a statue, or all three. The otherworldly animals, conjured out of the artist's imagination, reflect the heightened sense of reality that such ritual performances created.

With the development of a larger, more centralized state and the invention of writing that accompanied it, ancient Egyptians drew closely on their observations of the natural world to depict the divine one in art, including hieroglyphic signs. The animal world offered examples of behaviour that invited cosmic explanations, especially where an animal's actions seemed unusual (burying its eggs in dung, like a scarab-beetle) or miraculous (a bird in flight). From the most skilled, and secret, depictions that artists created on the walls of royal tombs, to the objects that magicians used in protective rites, animals were everywhere. Hippos, lions, jackals, all kinds of snakes, some remarkable reptiles, and a bewildering number of birds: you didn't need an actual zoo to perform Egyptian magic. But a small menagerie came in handy – or at least, some familiarity with the kinds of animals a magician might need to know and the powers they might help him channel.

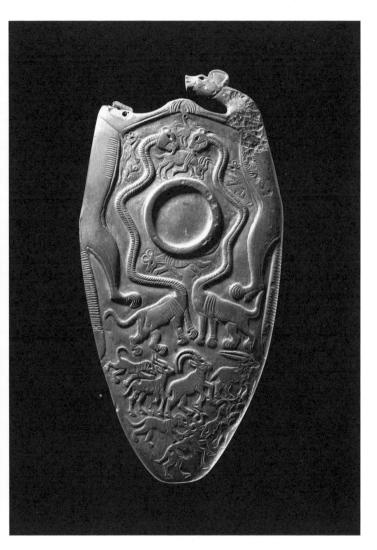

The 'Two-Dog Palette', a Predynastic example
of both real and fantastic animals in art.

Limestone stela of the craftsman Aa-pehty
praying to the god Seth, from Deir el-Medina.

Four-footed friends and fiends

The faience hippopotamus figures placed in Middle Kingdom burials still count as quadrupeds, even minus a foot. The hippo was feared in ancient times for the threat it posed to people working on or near the all-important marshes of the Nile. Its habit of moving between land and water, and cooling itself off with marshy, muddy baths, may have echoed Egyptian ideas about creation, many of which attributed primordial, life-giving powers to Nile water and Nile-drenched mud. But the hippo's dangerous side also encouraged its association with Seth, the brother (and murderer) of Osiris and the god blamed for natural disruptions like thunderstorms and earthquakes. As a symbol of such danger and disruption, the hippopotamus appears in many contexts as a hunted, wounded animal, because a conquered hippopotamus symbolized triumph over the forces of disorder – exactly the kind of metaphor a magician might want to call on in rites that aimed to right a wrong, heal the sick, or avert disaster. Objects made of hippopotamus ivory had special magical potency, including wands that were used for health and protection, especially during childbirth and the care of small children (for which see Chapter 6).

As a god of disorder on an almost inconceivable scale, threatening no less than the destruction of the natural order itself, it was fitting that Seth also had as his symbol an animal that was itself inconceivable. The 'Seth animal' (finally, Egyptology gives us a sensible term) was a four-legged creature with a down-turned snout, long ears with squared-off ends, and a tail that sometimes took the form of an arrow, as if pinning this weird creature down to stop it from causing havoc. The beast wasn't all bad, though: in the Delta during the New Kingdom, Seth also had a thriving cult that must have brought out his better side. He is honoured in the names of two 19th Dynasty kings, Sety I (r. *c.* 1323–1279 BCE) and Sety II (r. *c.* 1200–1194 BCE), whose family roots were in the region. Nevertheless, most magic spells that mention Seth were trying to curtail his negative influence.

The desert edges of the Nile valley were home to other wild animals whose ambiguous qualities – simultaneously feared and admired – made them ripe for magical interpretation, too. The jackal, for example, was identified with two gods who look almost the same in Egyptian art: Anubis, the jackal-headed god responsible for embalming and wrapping the corpse of Osiris, and Wepwawet, whose name means something like 'opener of the ways' or 'route-finder', making him a sort of sniffer dog to the supernatural realm. Jackals towed the sun-god's boat through the sky, their tails sometimes represented as rearing cobras. A jackal stretched out alert on top of a chest was the hieroglyphic sign for mastering secrecy, the vital skill that priest-magicians needed to perform effective rituals. It read *hery-seshta*, 'master of secrets', as written on the lid of the box in which the Ramesseum magician kept his papyri and magical kit.

A wooden jackal sculpture draped in layers of linen and adorned with a floral wreath was found on top of an actual chest inside Tutankhamun's tomb, guarding the innermost room. Inside the chest were numerous linen-wrapped objects: faience models in the shape of a meat joint (an ox-leg, for instance), *shabti*-figures (miniature mummies, who could be animated to provide labour in the afterlife), *djed*-amulets, a lump of resin, and jewelry or ornaments. These were almost certainly the remains of materials used in a ritual performance during Tutankhamun's funeral – the ultimate magic show, given that the death of a pharaoh meant that the fate of both king and country were at stake.

Opposite Wooden, linen-wrapped jackal on a shrine fitted with carrying poles, seen here as found in the tomb of Tutankhamun.

A wild cat kills a serpent in this modern copy of a painting
from the tomb of Sennedjem at Deir el-Medina.

As well as dogs, famously, the Egyptians worshipped cats, though perhaps less zealously than is popularly imagined. Both domesticated and wild cats were admired as hunters in ancient Egypt, and as we have seen hunting was a metaphor for overcoming dangerous forces. A tawny wildcat helped the sun-god defeat the evil serpent Apep, and in illustrated versions of the Book of the Dead, a cat looking rather pleased with itself slices a snake's body in two with a knife. The same collection includes a spell to animate a cat amulet, specified as being made of the blue stone lapis lazuli, although perhaps faience was more likely:

Oh cat of lapis lazuli, great of forms, mistress of the embalming house, grant offerings to So-and-so in the Beautiful West!

The 'Beautiful West' was the cemetery where the amulet's owner would be buried. Being 'great of forms' meant having multiple manifestations or *bau*, the spirit forms that were a sign of how powerful a god or a spirit was.

Cats were also linked to several goddesses, none more so than Bastet, who had a huge temple in her honour in the Delta. Like Sekhmet, Bastet protected the sun-god Ra. In fact, in her earliest forms, she too had a lioness's head. Later on, though, Bastet appeared in art as a beautiful woman with the head of a domesticated cat. Hundreds of bronze sculptures of cats were dedicated at shrines and temples in her honour, whether to help make a prayer, give thanks, or commemorate an event. Amulets of cats also proliferated, suggesting that the image of a cat had multiple uses as a protective or healing symbol. Without veterinary sterilization, a healthy female cat can give birth to a litter of kittens every few months. This made the cat a symbol of fertility and maternal care, as anyone who has seen a cat looking after her kittens can appreciate.

Leaded bronze statuette of a cat,
designed to hold a mummified kitten.

The flip side of feline fertility was that there were an awful lot of cats and kittens around in ancient Egypt. Thousands of mummified cats and kittens have been discovered in temple sites and cemeteries, where they were deposited as offerings to the gods. There are also a handful of examples of cats buried in their owners' tombs after a long, happy life; one, named Ta-Miaw ('The she-cat'), belonged to a son of King Amenhotep III and was buried in her own carved limestone coffin. However, most of these mummified moggies were hastened on their way to the afterlife by human hands – snapped necks or death by drowning gave embalmers the body they needed to make an attractively wrapped cat bundle. Alternatively, they made do without; some cat-shaped mummies contain no more than a mixture of earth and pebbles. It was the wrapping, and a priestly blessing, that mattered when it came to offering a cat mummy and asking for divine intervention. With a little magic, any of these sacred cat-shaped creatures might have done the trick.

The practice of dedicating mummified cats (and other animals) to the gods flourished from around 600 BCE into the Roman period – exactly the time when contact between Egypt and the northern Mediterranean was increasing. Greek and Roman authors who visited or read about Egypt were baffled by the Egyptians' fondness for cats, and we owe them several stories that sound like tall tales. In the 1st century CE, Diodorus of Sicily reported that killing a cat was a crime in Egypt, and claimed that a Roman official had been put to death by a mob for doing just that, back in the days of Cleopatra's father. The historian Polyaenus, writing in the 2nd century CE, stretched even further back in history for his cat-obsessed tale. When the Persian king Cambyses invaded Egypt around 525 BCE, Polyaenus wrote, he hit on a successful military tactic: the Persians placed cats all along their front lines, which stopped the Egyptian army from attacking for fear of causing harm to the tabby army.

The pharaoh himself could be represented as the most famous

Egyptian feline hybrid: the sphinx. We owe the name 'sphinx' to ancient Greek, however; there is no equivalent word in ancient Egyptian, because each sphinx simply represented a particular king. The massive sphinx that stands before the pyramids at Giza is an exception, since it came to be worshipped in its own right as a form of the sun-god. A sphinx had the body of a lion and a human head, covered by the pleated linen headdress called a *nemes*, worn by kings and associated with the radiant light of their divine nature.

Egyptian mythology included many other composite creatures based on lions, such as the ram-headed lions that lined the routes to temples. Two lions, back-to-back, with the sun rising or setting between them represented the god Aker, who guarded the western horizon – the entrance to the netherworld. One lion was named 'yesterday' and the other 'tomorrow'. Lions on their own also had protective qualities, and often appear in miniature form as amulets and on magical implements, like a carved stone rod or staff that seems to have been part of a magician's equipment. The lioness was not a force to be trifled with, either. Given to fury and foul moods, during which she brought disease to humankind, Ra's daughter Sekhmet always appeared with the head of a lioness. Offerings of beer and other treats helped to pacify her, while her priests worked hard to cure the various ailments she caused.

Magic rod carved with protective animals,
in glazed steatite.

Limestone stela honouring the sphinx-god
Tutu and the dwarf-god Bes.

Later in Egyptian history, a sphinx-shaped god named Tutu developed a popular following in several parts of Egypt, including the Dakhla Oasis, where settlement expanded under Roman rule. With knives in his paws and solar rays streaming from his head, Tutu was known as the 'master of demons'. Thanks to his demon-driving powers and knife-wielding form, Egyptologists used to assume that Tutu was a sort of demi-god or demon himself, who could be called on in magic spells. More recent research suggests something quite different, however. Tutu seems to have in fact been a manifestation, or *bau*, of the solar creator-god Amun-Ra, and images of Tutu appear mainly inside temples, rather than in domestic contexts or among magic spells and equipment. As a mighty god who could control demons, perhaps he was too frightening a figure for a magician to call on directly. In any case, confusion over Tutu's role underscores

The cobra-goddess Wadjet and vulture-goddess Nekhbet,
protectors of the king.

the difficulty of separating magic from other religious practices in our interpretation of ancient culture. We can only understand magic and myth, not to mention art and religion, as interconnecting parts of a supernatural whole.

Slippery snakes and other raucous reptiles

Snakes are the animals most frequently encountered in Egyptian magic, from the wands or staffs that magicians used in magic rites, to the variety of gods, demi-gods, and demons described and depicted in snake form. With its distinctive sideways locomotion, habit of appearing silently and suddenly, and a dangerous, potentially lethal, bite, the snake epitomized danger. No wonder Apep, arch-enemy of Ra, took the form of a gigantic serpent slithering through the Duat, and Isis enchanted a wax snake to inject venom into Ra to learn his secret name.

Because snakes were so formidable, they could also channel the forces of protection. Hence the fiery-mouthed cobras placed at the four corners of a room to ward off nightmares, as we saw in the last chapter. Of all the snakes known to the ancient Egyptians, the hooded cobra was especially significant. The cobra was an aspect of the sun and thus embodied its powerful heat, emitting venomous flames to save the king, magically, from harm. As the *uraeus* on the king's forehead, the cobra represented Wadjet, a Delta-based goddess who was one of the two traditional goddesses who protected the pharaoh. (The other was Nekhbet, from the south of the country, who was shown instead as a vulture.)

Many other goddesses took the form of snakes as well. The goddess Renenutet, associated with agricultural fertility, often had the body of a cobra, while Meretseger, 'she who loves silence', sometimes appeared as a cobra and sometimes as a woman with a cobra's head. Meretseger was worshipped on the distinctive pyramid-shaped mountain that overlooks the cemeteries on the West Bank of the Nile at Thebes (modern Luxor). This goddess seems also to have had associations with fertility and nourishment. An unusually high number of dedications made to her at the village of Deir el-Medina were donated by women, including a stela that represents a dozen slithering snakes in place of a human figure of the goddess. The stela's prayer is in honour of Wab, the woman shown kneeling at the bottom.

Another reptilian creature, the crocodile, inspired endless magical actions and myths. Moving between the water and the land, crocodiles occupied a similar borderland to hippopotami in the ancient Egyptian imagination, and they could similarly be friend or foe. Crocodiles are extraordinarily dangerous creatures, with even a young adult capable of killing a human in minutes. In tomb paintings that show vulnerable, precious cattle crossing a canal, a crocodile often lurks threateningly below the water line. The herdsmen have a magician to help with that, however. He makes a magical hand gesture (two fingers pointing out, and two folded into the palm) and recites a water spell to protect the herdsmen and their cattle from the 'marsh-dweller' by rendering the crocodile blind.

Warding off the crocodile meant warding off death itself, given the killing power of these swift-moving reptiles. But turn that murderous power to your own ends, through magic, and crocodiles came in handy, as we saw in Chapter 1, where two drawings of crocodiles completed the folded-up papyrus amulet a magician had made for his client. These drawings may evoke one of the beneficent crocodile gods, of whom Sobek was the most widely known and worshipped, especially in the Fayum region. One temple in the Fayum Oasis honoured twin crocodile gods who were identified, in Roman times, with the youthful Horus and his father Osiris. Priests of Sobek raised crocodiles in temple quarters, and young mummified crocodiles served as sacred offerings, in much the same way as cat mummies. So much better than turning them into shoes and handbags.

Stela dedicated by Nebnefer to Meretseger, a cobra-goddess
identified with the highest mountain of Thebes.

Above The constellation Ursa Major, here associated
with a hippo-goddess, from the Book of the Fayum.

Opposite The crocodile-god Sobek,
from the Book of the Fayum.

The crocodile was the most recognizable, and deadly, part of the hybrid creature called Ammut (literally, 'devourer of the dead'), who was depicted slavering expectantly near the balance scales during the weighing of the dead person's heart in the judgment ceremony. Ammet had the head of a crocodile, the mane and foreparts of a lion, and the rump of a hippopotamus. Another crocodile hybrid had an entirely different, more peaceable character, however. Taweret – literally, 'the Great One' – had a hippopotamus body with the paws of a wild cat and the tail of a crocodile. Taweret always appeared standing upright on her hind legs like a human, with breasts that had been stretched out by nursing babies. This gives a clue to Taweret's role as a deity who protected expectant mothers and young children, as does the *sa*-hieroglyph she often rests her front paws on. Taweret carries protection before her, like an amulet within the amulet of her own incredible animal form.

A monstrous-looking body did not mean that a supernatural being had a monstrous character. Quite the opposite was often true. A similar-looking figure to Taweret, with an entire crocodile forming her backbone, was identified with the constellation we know as the Great Bear (Ursa Major) and with the goddesses Ipet, Neith, and

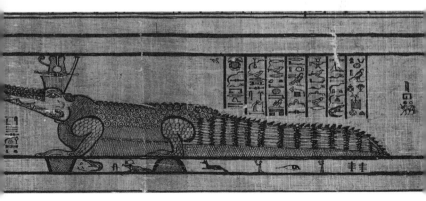

Nut, all of whom also had special connections with motherhood and birth. The crocodile on the back of this Ipet/Great Bear goddess was a fusion of Sobek and Ra, and it was through her mighty body that these creator-gods could be reborn as they travelled through the starry night.

Crawling critters

It wasn't all hefty hippos and lordly lions for an Egyptian magician. He had to be able to deal with much smaller creatures, too. One of the most common amulets found in faience or carved stone is the scarab, a beetle with the distinctive habit of laying its eggs in dung, which it then rolled into a ball to nurture them into life. This action might have led ancient Egyptians to associate the scarab with the sun, so that the scarab was often shown holding or pushing the solar disk between its front legs. The scarab developed its own layers of mythology over time. The god Osiris was said to have a scarab beetle under his head, which emerged with wings that allowed it to fly up into the sky – a sign of his regeneration. In magic, a scarab could be worn as an amulet or used with mud, clay, or wax as a seal, for instance to close a roll of papyrus or the looped cord that held two doors or a lid closed shut. Sealing brought together the magical tools of writing and secrecy, and seals were also made in the form of hedgehogs and hares, creatures that could also possess protective powers, it seems.

In contrast to scarab beetles, which are overwhelmingly positive symbols, the scorpion was always bad news. Scorpion stings are rarely, if ever, life-threatening, but they are extremely painful. As we saw in Chapter 2, magicians known as scorpion-charmers accompanied mining expeditions into the desert, where scorpions were a professional hazard. Associated with the goddess Serket (or Selket), the scorpion symbolized all kinds of pain and suffering, and magical exhortations aimed at overcoming the scorpion's sting

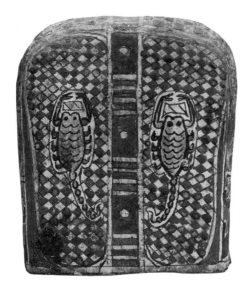

Scorpions on the underside of a mummy's footcase
would be trampled and magically defeated.

were no doubt meant to keep a range of troubles at bay. The child
Horus grasped scorpions in his hands to demonstrate his power
over them as a symbol of his rightful dominion over the cosmos,
while the soles of some mummy cases depicted scorpions that the
deceased would crush safely underfoot, thereby defeating evil and
overcoming death itself.

Feathered friends

Although feathers are not explicitly called for in magic spells as a
tool or an ingredient, you couldn't move in the supernatural world
of ancient Egypt without feeling, hearing, or seeing the swoosh of a
bird's wing. Birds are not really of this world, after all. Their ability
to fly, their brightly coloured plumage, and the sound of their calls,

singly or en masse, all made birds seem like messengers from another world. Egyptian texts compared the colour of birds' feathers to the spectrum of the sun's rays. The graceful, encompassing curve and flare of outstretched wings gave artists and magicians alike a perfect symbol for other-worldly powers of protection, while the beating of wings in flight captured the sensation of a breeze or wind, both natural phenomena that might signal supernatural presence. The creator-god Amun of Thebes was credited as 'master of the winds' in magic spells written during Ptolemaic and Roman times, but the idea had much earlier roots. The magician-priest prayed to Amun, 'ruler of all', in order to access the powers of creation that wind – and by extension, wings – represented.

The spirit forms of human beings could take flight, too. The *ba* of a person who had died was represented as a bird with a human head. If the magic performed during mummification and burial had worked, the *ba* could fly out of the tomb by day, returning to the mummified body each night for a cosmic reunion and renewal. The most elevated spirit-forms of the dead, the *akhu*, were represented by the hieroglyphic sign of a crested ibis. The *akhu* were 'the luminous ones', associated with dazzling light. Being a bird really was divine.

Other birds that appeared frequently in Egyptian art and on magical objects were the vulture, which was associated with the goddesses Nekhbet and Mut, and the African sacred ibis, which was always identified with Thoth. Hundreds of thousands of mummified ibises were dedicated at temples, stacked in special underground chambers along with mummies of Thoth's other sacred animal, the baboon. As with the kittens and young crocodiles that were mummified as offerings, these birds and baboons met premature deaths in order to serve what was, to the ancient Egyptians who donated them, a higher good.

Birds of prey – specifically the falcon and the red kite – brought to divine symbolism the added appeal of their impressive speed and

The priest Padihorsiese dedicated this bronze ibis to Thoth.

hunting ability. Ra and Horus are the two male deities best known for taking falcon form, but there were many more. The temple of Horus at Edfu kept a sacred falcon in a specially built cage high up on the temple gateway. His mother Isis and her sister Nephthys instead took the form of red kites. The keening cries of these birds were likened to the wails the two sisters made as they mourned the murder of their brother Osiris. Isis sometimes took the form of a kite during the mystical love-making that allowed her to conceive Horus from Osiris's reinvigorated dead body.

Many goddesses, especially Isis, Nephthys, and the sky-goddess Nut, had outstretched wings added to their human arms when they were represented in art. So, too, did Maat, the goddess who personified truth and cosmic justice, against whom – in the form of a single feather – the deceased were judged. Overlapping wings painted onto coffins, or stretched around the corners of sarcophagi, brought magical protection to the person buried inside. Feather patterns on garments and furniture must have had a similar function, as well as giving everything they adorned a bright, blazing appearance.

Above Red kites representing Nephthys (left) and Isis (right),
either side of a wrapped mummy in the tomb of Queen Nefertari.

Opposite Fragment of papyrus with a magician's drawing
of a winged god surrounded by protective flames.

Wings were often attached to animals who didn't actually have them on amulets, in particular the scarab and the ram, both of which were aspects of the sun god and thus perfectly suited to the feathery symbolism of sunlight, colour, and air. A sheet of papyrus probably cut from a magician's handbook shows the extent to which bird anatomy contributed to the perception of the supernatural. From a human body, a figure sprouts two pairs of arms and two sets of wings, as well as the tail-end of a bird. He holds *was*-sceptres that symbolize power and some lethal-looking arrows and knives. The creature also has several animal heads, including lions, crocodiles, and rams, and his body is covered with protective knots. Individual flames surround the entire figure, and he stands – with serpent-shaped feet – on a ring that encloses several harmful forces: a scorpion, snakes, a crocodile, two jackals, and a pig, the pig being another animal that was associated with Seth. Although the rest of the papyrus isn't preserved, this illustration may have been part of a handbook of spells, used to help a magician conjure a god whose formidable hybrid appearance would work to defend the magician and his client. In the magical menagerie of ancient Egypt, feathers were a magician's best friend.

OH, THE SNAKE BITES...

... with its teeth, dear, and when it does it would be good to have some magic to hand. Likewise for scorpion stings, stomachaches, itchy eyes, a sore head, and any unexplained swelling or bleeding. For anything that ails you, in fact, because magic was the first line of defence against diseases in ancient Egypt, as well as the best chance of a cure. Most people relied on a combination of magical charms and simple practices such as cleaning a wound, applying an ointment, or ingesting whatever concoction your local magician offered to stay healthy. Recovery was proof that the magic had worked, while for those who never recovered, well, that was proof that the demons who caused disease were very powerful indeed.

Modern medical studies of the placebo effect – when patients respond well to taking pills that contain no active ingredients – have demonstrated that believing in the power of a cure can be just as effective as the cure itself. Strange as ancient healing magic may seem from our vantage point today, we shouldn't assume that it was useless. Like other magic spells, those designed to treat injury or illness often came with assurances that they were tried-and-tested, top-secret remedies. 'Very effective! It's worked a thousand times!' was often written at the end of a healing spell, like a quality mark for wizardry.

Such spells were collected together on papyrus scrolls, sometimes organized by ailment (snake bites, eye problems, and what used to be known euphemistically as 'female problems'), and sometimes mixed in with other kinds of magical invocations. In early studies of these papyri, Egyptologists tried to separate the diagnosis of a problem from the suggested cure, because the act of diagnosing an ailment seemed more like modern medicine, whereas the cures clearly prescribed a magical action. To understand how the Egyptians approached the art of healing, however, we have to abandon that kind of distinction. Magic and medicine went together like deep-fried catfish and a headache: rub your head with the oil in which the head of a catfish has been fried, and see if that doesn't offer some relief. Or at least a little something to snack on.

Protecting yourself against falling ill in the first place was also crucial, as we know from spells for the wearing of amulets, but when things did go wrong, a magician had several options at his disposal to try to combat the demonic forces thought to cause disease. The story of Horus's childhood was one such source of healing inspiration – for a magical child living under divine protection, he ran into an awful lot of trouble, and his mother constantly had to use her powers to heal him or save him from one threat or another. Priests in the service of the lion-goddess Sekhmet were the nearest equivalent to modern doctors, but other magicians offered healing services as well. Some men became so famous for their healing powers that they were honoured as gods, like the priest Imhotep, whose name has been kept alive in Victorian mummy fiction and Hollywood films. Appealing to Imhotep for his divine help may have been the last resort for families struck down by the kinds of infectious diseases for which there was no cure but a prayer – and a wing.

The magical child

At the end of the last chapter, we met a triumphant and ferocious winged figure, treading his serpent-feet over the successfully corralled animals of evil. A similar figure appears in many contexts connected to protective magic and healing practices, under different names

The Metternich Stela: a high-quality healing monument
set up in a temple *c.* 360–343 BCE.

(or no name at all) and on objects made in a range of materials, from faience amulets to top-quality carved stone monuments. One such monument is a Horus-on-the-crocodiles cippus known as the Metternich Stela, after the Austrian diplomat Prince von Metternich-Winneberg, to whom it was given by the ruler of Egypt, Mohammed Ali, in 1828. Standing around 84 centimetres (33 inches) high, the stela once stood inside a temple dedicated to the sacred Mnevis bull, which was connected to the worship of Ra at Heliopolis. The stela was set up by a priest named Nesu-Atum during the reign of King Nectanebo II (*c.* 350 BCE), in order to offer healing magic to people who came to the temple to seek the help of priests, magicians, and healers like Nesu-Atum. Like the statue of the priests of Bastet (see page 59), the Metternich Stela was incised on every surface with magical figures and spells that offered healing and protection. No one but a priest would have been able to read the spells or explain in any detail the imagery alongside them. But the presence of the spells and images together was essential to the stela's power. Water poured over them would absorb the words, and those who drank the water took that magic into their own bodies, in hope of the relief of whatever ailed them.

The winged figure with a bird's tail, human body, and the face of Bes has pride of place on the back of the stela, which was no less important than the other sides in terms of how this object functioned. Like a healing statue, the stela was designed so that each side of it was visible and accessible, perhaps for people to walk around as part of their cure. The word for a remedy was *pekher*, 'to encircle' or 'to go around', the same as the word for magical enchantment. As with the use of knotted loops to protect royal names, or of oval enclosures to contain harmful forces, circular motions helped activate the magic in ancient Egyptian practice.

The visual focus on the front of the Metternich Stela is the Horus-on-the-crocodiles scene itself, carved in a rectangular recess. Young Horus, the magical child, stands in a shelter with the protective

Top Upper part of the back of the Metternich Stela: a winged god surrounded by protective flames, with rows of deities beneath.

Above The main scene on the front of the Metternich Stela: Horus-on-the-crocodiles is protected by the head of Bes.

face of Bes overhead and a pair of contrite-looking crocodiles under-foot. Horus has the pudgy body and side-lock of hair that were common to Egyptian depictions of children. His nakedness also is a sign that he is only an infant or toddler, since a lack of clothing symbolized the early stages of human development. In his hands he grasps a lion by its tail, an antelope by its horns, two scorpions, and a pair of snakes, which between them represent harmful, inhos-pitable forces. On either side of Horus's shelter we see his mother Isis and the god Thoth, each standing upon a subdued snake. Inside the shelter are Ra-Horakhty, god of the setting sun, and a symbol of the god Nefertum, consisting of a lotus blossom and two upright feathers. At the far ends of the recess, the same vulture and cobra goddesses that protected the pharaoh – Nekhbet and Wadjet – protect the entire composition, as do the right- and left-facing *wedjat*-eyes over the enclosure. The *wedjat* is more commonly known as the 'Eye of Horus'; according to an ancient legend, Seth tried to blind his nephew by piercing or gouging out this eye, but either Thoth or Hathor (depending on the source) used magic to return it and restore his sight. His eyes became linked with the sun (right) and moon (left),

A gold cover for the embalming incision of King Psusennes II's mummy shows the Four Sons of Horus standing on either side of the *wedjat*-eye.

and so were potent symbols of regeneration; paired *wedjat*-eyes on the sides of some coffins magically let the deceased person's mummy see through the coffin walls. The sculptor has thus employed rich symbolism over every part of the recessed area to convey the cosmic space that the deities inhabit, just as he used every part of the stela's surface for the emblems and spells that were also essential to its magical function.

Because the Metternich Stela has been known to Egyptologists for a long time, and because its inscriptions are so well-preserved, it has served as a model for scholars studying this variety of healing spells. Similar spells are known from many other sources as well, ranging from inscriptions carved on temple walls to handbooks written on papyrus, suggesting that these were reasonably familiar in ancient Egyptian society. They take us to the heart of the story of Horus and his mother Isis, at a point in mythical time that falls after Seth's murder of Osiris and before Horus has grown up to avenge his father and regain the throne of Egypt. Mythical time means that all these events can exist at once. The story of Isis and the infant Horus set a divine precedent for healing magic (as well as assistance with childbirth, as we'll see in the next chapter). Mother and child lived in hiding from Seth, taking refuge in the remote marshes of the Delta. There, Isis struggled to nourish young Horus and keep him healthy – something we can imagine so many Egyptian mothers identified with, given the high rate of infant and child mortality in ancient societies.

The Isis spells on the Metternich Stela recount two versions of a story in which children are stung by scorpions, accompanied by spells to help rid a child of poison. In the first version, Isis has tamed seven scorpions to help protect her and Horus. When the scorpions bite another woman's son, however, Isis uses her power to call the poison out of the child's body and save him: 'May the child live and the poison die', goes the incantation that accompanies this story, 'and those who suffer will be cured likewise.'

In the second version, the young Horus has become the victim of a scorpion sting, challenging even Isis's powers of healing. She halts the sun-god's boat as it crosses the sky above, bringing time to a standstill. Ra sends ibis-headed Thoth, god of wisdom, to answer Isis's call for help (and to get his boat moving again). 'Awake, Horus,' says Thoth. 'I am Thoth sent to cure you for your mother Isis, and I cure the suffering person likewise. May the poison die, may its fire be extinguished.'

Both of these stories, with their healing refrains, illustrate an important principle of medical magic: identification with the gods. The magician pronouncing the spell took on the identity of the healing god, here Isis or Thoth, while the afflicted person was identified with the ailing child. We are all vulnerable, like a child, when we are suffering and unwell. By establishing a divine precedent for recovery, these healing formulas offered reassurance that the cure would work – or at least, that the patient was in the gods' hands. And although the Isis-and-Horus stories focus on scorpion stings and snake bites, we should not assume that these were the only problems these spells could treat. Although snake venom and some scorpion stings could kill, and were clearly a concern (one papyrus contains hundreds of spells against snake bites), it makes more sense to see them as metaphors for a host of aches, pains, itches, and fevers. Wellness in general seems to have been the greater aim, which chimes with the extremely high quality and privileged position such objects had inside temple enclosures.

Portable magic

What if you were too ill, or too far away, to get to a temple and benefit from the effects of a professionally made healing stela or statue in its prestigious, sacred setting? Fortunately, Egyptian magic still had you covered. Your local amulet-maker, scorpion-charmer, or priest of Sekhmet was usually happy to make home visits. Magicians who had trained as priests almost certainly adapted the rituals they learned inside the temple to contexts outside of it. A magician with a particular knack for cures might have developed a loyal following in his own community and as far afield as he, or his patients, could travel. We can also imagine that healers with little or no formal training – including women – likewise borrowed or adapted more widely known rites to their personal practice. Every experienced magician brings his (or her) own secrets and skills to bear.

The fact that magic can happen almost anywhere is one of its strengths, after all, and nothing demonstrates that more than wearable or portable objects connected to cures and protection from illness. Carved versions of the Horus-on-the-crocodiles motif that fit in the hand, or were even smaller, allowed the healing power of image, words, and action to reach more people, in more ways. Hundreds, if not thousands, of amulets depicting the Horus scene survive in museum collections, often with a hole that allowed them to be hung on a cord and worn on the body. Many of the wearable or portable Horus objects and amulets either lack inscribed spells, or have such cramped, illegible, or even imitation inscriptions that the image itself must have contained adequate magical power, together with the words the healer recited over it.

Amulets made of coloured stones or shiny blue-green faience are the most numerous magical objects, by far, from ancient Egypt – but they are also among the most easily overlooked, both because of their small size and because there are so many of them. Admittedly, some are more arresting to look at than others. But looks mattered less than what the amulet was capable of. Diminutive size didn't make an object less powerful; in fact, it could make it easier to hide, and as we know secrecy was vital to effective magic. Moreover, amulets worn in direct contact with the body had an intimate, personal power to protect and support the wearer. Not all amulets were made of stone or faience. A magical text or drawing made on a piece of papyrus and folded up tightly worked just as well when it came from the hands of a magician, accompanied by his incantations. Such amulets, or little cases to contain them, often appear at the throats of small children in mummy portraits from Roman Egypt. These portraits were embedded in the wrappings of the children's mummies, and cynics may say this casts doubt on how effective the amulet had been. To look at it another way, placing a healing amulet, or an image of the amulet, onto the deceased's body extended the amulet's power into the next world, in hopes that the child would find the long life there that it was not granted in this one.

Mummy portrait of a young boy
wearing an amulet at his throat.

Knotting magic was used for healing magic, too, however unimpressive a knotted length of cord, papyrus, or linen may look. The knots locked in the words a magician spoke during a healing rite, as one spell against a headache describes. In the spell, the magician assumed the role of Seth and the suffering person became Horus – proof that Seth had his uses. The magician ('Seth') recited the healing words while tying knots into a cord, which was then placed around the foot of 'Horus'. Lengths of knotted cloth or papyrus that survive in museum collections must be the physical remains of similar practices. Magic made simple was no less powerful.

If you believed, that is. Much of the effectiveness of medical magic depended on placebo power, or at best some basic first aid and the healing effects of time. Any amulet, and the incantations that empowered it, could only do so much in the face of many of the illnesses we know that ancient Egyptians suffered, in particular any kind of viral or bacterial infection, as well as cancerous growths, thyroid problems, and eye infections. Before the discovery of antibiotics and other drug therapies in the 20th century, such conditions were always difficult, if not impossible, to treat. Fortunately, spells and amulets weren't the only tricks of the healer's trade in ancient Egypt. Magicians also knew how to mix up medicine, although whether you'd want to take it was another question.

An Egyptian herbal

Pity the poor patient whose healer chanted this spell in order to convince them to swallow some medicine:

> Here is the medicine to dispel bad substances from my
> heart and limbs. *Heka* is strong because of this medicine,
> and this medicine is strong because of *heka*. Do you

remember when Horus and Seth were taken to the Great
Palace of Heliopolis for an inquiry into Seth's testicles?
After that, Horus flourished like a living person; he could
do anything he wanted, just like the gods.

Notes for the magician praise this formula as 'a true method, proved
an infinite number of times', another common quality assurance at
the end of magic spells and remedies. An infinite number of times
adds up to quite a lot of testicles.

You might prefer a spoonful of honey to an incantation that men-
tions Seth's private parts. But the spell has prestigious precedents. It
refers to a group of very old myths, some of which were collected on
a papyrus written around 1100 BCE and known as 'The Contendings
of Horus and Seth'. According to these myths, a tribunal of gods at
Heliopolis, the home of the cult of Ra, called Horus and Seth to appear
before them in order to put an end to their conflict over the throne
of Osiris. In the magic spell quoted above, Seth's testicles (or semen,
perhaps) may allude to an episode in the 'Contendings' when Seth
sexually assaulted his nephew. The gods' final verdict vindicated
Horus, which restored him – and in the magic spell, the patient – to
wholeness and health.

Strikingly, the spell equates *heka*, or magic, with the medicine the
patient needs to swallow, and vice versa. Consuming the medicine
meant consuming its *heka*, which in turn would put an end to the
patient's suffering; it's similar to the principle of absorption that
saw Setne dissolve a copy of the Book of Thoth and drink it. The
spell is less specific about what the patient's exact symptoms were.
Perhaps a general sense of feeling weak and unwell was the problem,
here attributed to bad or unbalanced substances among the inner
workings of the body.

Most magical remedies were based on plant sources, using the
seeds, fruits, flowers, and leaves from many herbs, shrubs, and trees

still familiar to us today. Ground into a paste or powder, and sometimes left to soak up life-giving dew overnight, plant ingredients were combined with water, honey, milk, animal fat, or vegetable oil to make up a versatile mixture. Swallowing it down wasn't the only way these prescriptions were administered: depending on the complaint, the mixture might be applied directly to the body as a poultice, ointment, or eye wash. Egyptian healers were fond of a pessary or suppository for complaints 'down there', and they also burned ingredients to fumigate a space, whether to cleanse it of impurities, cause the patient to inhale therapeutic substances, or both. Medicine that did have to be ingested often included wine or beer in the mixture. Even if there were no other active ingredients in the concoction, the patient at least had the consolation of an alcohol-based swig.

Ancient Egyptian healing concoctions did contain active ingredients, in keeping with herbal medical practices the world over. 'Folk' knowledge passed on through generations recognized the astringent, diuretic, laxative, purgative, stimulating, or pain-relieving qualities of different plants – like the notoriously bitter leaves of wormwood (*Artemisia absinthium*), which may owe its common English name to its traditional effectiveness against intestinal worms. A cure for pain in the rectum (caused, of course, by a demon) called for a compound of wormwood, juniper berries, honey, and beer to be passed through a sieve and consumed for four consecutive days. Another remedy for worms required a tincture of acacia leaves, which are known for their astringent properties. Ancient Egyptian magical-medical texts also recommend a paste of ground-up acacia leaves for the treatment of open sores and even broken bones. The leaves and berries of willow and Christ-thorn (*Zizyphus*) trees, known to have pain-relieving effects, occur in a many prescriptions, as do myrtle leaves, which have some antiseptic properties. Also making a regular appearance in ancient prescriptions are the leaves, flowers, and seeds of the marshmallow plant; the pods and gum of the carob tree; and celery, which could be mixed up with beer to make a chew-and-spit substance that was said to relieve tooth pain.

One mixture that probably did offer mild pain relief and speed up the healing of skin wounds was a poultice of ground linseeds from the flax plant, an important crop in ancient Egypt valued for its seeds, oil, and use in the production of linen. The ancient Egyptians also understood the soothing properties of aloe on burns and skin inflammations, and probably used it as a purgative as well. Cleaning the body from the inside out was often the first recourse a healer had when faced with a patient's internal aches and pains. Castor-oil would get things moving through one end of the digestive tract or the other, and the ancient Egyptians were no strangers to the laxative qualities of figs. Another suggestion for clearing the bowels required a paste of ground carob and beer, which was mixed with milk, honey, tiger nuts, and wine, then boiled, strained, and drunk for four days.

Several herbs with a culinary use did double duty in healing: dill in a recipe for a pain-soothing drink, fennel as a diuretic to help with bladder complaints, and cumin, which has stimulating properties, in cough remedies, tooth powders, and anal suppositories. Writing in the 1st century CE, the Roman writer Pliny the Elder praised the unsurpassed quality of several Egyptian herbs, including coriander. The seeds and leaves of this aromatic plant are called for in Egyptian prescriptions for stomach ailments and in an ointment possibly used against herpes or another sexually transmitted disease: mix ground coriander seeds, powdered myrrh, and honey, apply to the affected organ, and try not to stick to anything while this does (or doesn't) do its work.

Before you get too comfortable with the thought of antiseptic honey, chocolatey carob, and all that pharmaceutical beer and wine, be aware that some magical-medical spells call for less appetizing ingredients. Ancient Egyptian healing magic also made liberal use of the dung, bile, and blood of various animals, plus boiled human urine. Fortunately, most of the recipes that call for these ingredients used them externally, or at worst by inserting them into a patient's nether regions. Eye diseases were a common complaint in ancient Egypt, and one remedy to combat blindness called for a mixture of ground leeks and fresh urine to be applied regularly to the eyes. The Greek traveller Herodotus wrote about the medical use of urine after his visit to Egypt in the 5th century BCE, claiming that only the urine of a woman who hadn't deceived her husband would make the prescription work. Venture some misogynistic humour yourself, if your patients don't respond to treatment.

Some discussions of ancient Egyptian medicine have taken every ingredient at face value. One author reports in good faith a remedy for hair loss that called for the fat of a lion, a hippopotamus, a crocodile, a wildcat, a snake, and an ibex to be mixed together and applied as a pomade to the bald person's head. This sounds more like the original snake-oil sales pitch. The unlikely-sounding list of ingredients was surely meant to convince patients that they were getting something extra-exotic, and therefore extra-effective. There is often more to a magical remedy than meets the eye; strange or stomach-churning names helped amplify and mystify the magical power of more mundane ingredients, as we know from a bilingual Greek and Egyptian papyri composed during Roman times. The papyrus contains a handy glossary of ingredients, which informed magicians that a snake's head was in fact a leech, its blood was red ochre, and an ibis bone was the buckthorn plant. Baboon blood could more easily be retrieved from a spotted gecko, while baboon tears and hair-of-baboon were simply a bit of dill from the garden, squeezed into a juice or gathered from the seed heads. Unsure how to extract human bile without having to kill someone? Never fear: it's just turnip sap. Bodily liquids like blood and semen feature prominently in this magical recipe book, but they usually turn out to mean something else, such as clover, houseleek, lupin, or fleabane – and thank goodness for that. Crocodile dung makes an appearance, but since that's an expression for Ethiopian soil (which still sounds pretty exotic), it should be easier to come by.

Magic works by obscuring its methods and means. When it came to making, and taking, your medicine in ancient Egypt, magicians were doing exactly that. Giving smelly or impure substances repulsive labels made the cure seem terribly complicated and mysterious. But revulsion also inverted the natural order of things, mimicking the disorderly forces that had caused the illness or injury in the first place. Any healer worth his or her natron-salt would be able to turn those forces of disorder around to face the right direction, or so their anxious clients must have hoped. Inevitably, many of the illnesses an ancient Egyptian would face would lead to lifelong problems – or a hastened death. In extreme cases, appealing to the great healers of the past offered the only hope for those who had exhausted all the healers of the present.

Medicine men: Imhotep and Amenhotep

In the provincial town of Thebes during the reign of Emperor Trajan, a leading family lost two of its children to illness within a short time of each other. A son named Padiamenipet was nineteen years old when he died in 116 CE, and a daughter named Kleopatra was just seventeen; her exact date of death is unknown. Brother and sister were buried with almost identical mummification rites, their bodies wrapped in painted shrouds and placed in two similarly painted coffins. The coffins and mummy of Padiamenipet are now in the Louvre museum in Paris, while those of Kleopatra are in the British Museum in London. Their mummified bodies show no trace of trauma or obvious signs of disease, and indeed, many infectious diseases would not leave an obvious trace on the body. For two otherwise healthy members of a family to die in adolescence, an illness such as influenza, some form of plague, or perhaps tuberculosis may be the most likely explanations.

It also seems likely that the families of Padiamenipet and Kleopatra would have turned to healing magic for help, just like generations of Egyptians before them. Each sibling's coffin gives us a clue about what kind of help was sought – or more precisely, whose help, since on the outside wall of each coffin, at the head end, are painted two of the most famous healers from ancient Egypt: the wise Imhotep and a man named Amenhotep, son of Hapu, who was also credited with great wisdom and medical knowledge.

Both of these men were historical figures and both became worshipped as gods or, at the very least, demi-gods who could intercede between mortal humans and the divine realm. We've already met Imhotep, who lived in the reign of the 3rd Dynasty King Djoser (c. 2600 BCE) and has variously been credited as an architect, a physician, and a polymath. Originally based at Saqqara, the worship of Imhotep became widespread throughout Egypt, and thousands of bronze statuettes representing him survive. Less familiar today is Amenhotep, son of Hapu, so called to distinguish him from all the other men named Amenhotep – notably the kings – who lived, like him, during the late 18th Dynasty. At Thebes, Amenhotep lived a long, esteemed life, directing building projects for King Amenhotep III (r. c. 1386–1349 BCE). In return, the king allowed Amenhotep to erect statues of himself in the temple of Amun at Karnak. Some of these statues stood outside the temple gateways for centuries, inviting local people to pray to Amenhotep, son of Hapu, who would make sure the gods heard them. The statues show Amenhotep in the cross-legged posture of a dedicated scribe, with a roll of papyrus stretched across his lap. The stone surface has worn away over time as thousands of people touched the 'papyrus' to make contact with these statues as they prayed or passed by.

Coffin of a young woman named Kleopatra, showing
the healers Imhotep and Amenhotep, son of Hapu.

In the Ptolemaic Period, Imhotep and Amenhotep formed a healing pair in several temples in and around Thebes. In scenes carved on temple walls they were depicted as two respectable priests, Imhotep with a skull cap or closely shaved head and Amenhotep with a shoulder-length hairstyle or head-covering. The temples honoured both men as priests, magicians, and medical men, summing up the role of a priest-magician in ancient Egypt, and perhaps not far off the status these men had held in their own lifetimes.

Bronze statuette of Imhotep, who was worshipped
as a wise man, healer, and magician.

The coffins of Padiamenipet and Kleopatra depict Imhotep and Amenhotep in pride of place at the head end, either side of a boat in which the sun-god appears as a scarab beetle, protectively encircled by a snake that is swallowing its own tail. The specific inspiration for these coffin scenes is probably the temple of Hathor at Deir el-Medina, where Imhotep and Amenhotep are carved into columns inside the entrance. The two healing gods also appear in a temple of Thoth at nearby Qasr el-Aguz, and they had their own dedicated sanctuary just over the cliffs at Deir el-Bahri, where graffiti from the Roman period give thanks for healing and protection. The Deir el-Bahri sanctuary may have offered sleeping spaces where the faithful could spend the night, hoping for a message from the gods in their dreams. Any diagnosis and remedy received in this way would be considered especially potent, coming as it did straight from these deified doctor-priests.

Did Padiamenipet, Kleopatra, or members of their family go to one of these sanctuaries to seek healing from Imhotep and Amenhotep – and perhaps even try the sacred sleep of the Deir el-Bahri sanctuary? There's no way to know for certain, but the coffin paintings are so unusual that it seems a real possibility. In a world where magic and medicine went hand-in-hand, to represent these illustrious, ancestral medicine men alongside the scarab of the sun god, nearly cradling the head of the mummy itself, reminds us that healing the body and healing the soul were intimately related, in life and in death. Neither Padiamenipet nor Kleopatra survived their illnesses, but that doesn't mean they hadn't received some divine assistance from Imhotep and Amenhotep, son of Hapu, along the way. Ancient Egyptian magic could never guarantee a cure. But for those who believed in its power, magic could go a long way towards soothing a troubled heart.

6

LOVE, SEX, BABIES

There was another kind of heartache magic promised to help with, too – good old-fashioned lovesickness. If you wanted to make someone fall in love with you, or stay in love with you, there was a magic spell for that. Likewise if you wanted to get even with someone who had spurned your affections, or the rival who had captured their heart. One magical handbook includes a recipe for making the hair of a hated woman fall out: boil the seeds of a blue lotus, steep them in vegetable oil, and find an excuse for rubbing it into her head. There seem to have been fewer options for magical revenge on fickle men. Ancient Egypt was a patriarchal culture, and male magicians, priests, and scribes were responsible for almost all the written records that survive. Let's just hope that Egyptian women had other means of sharing effective curses with each other. A recipe to make a man go bald would certainly be a good start, although time often offers that particular salve.

We get a better idea of how women used magic when we look at fertility, pregnancy, childbirth, and caring for infants. Although the written evidence for these practices also comes from sources largely created by men, we know that it was women who assisted other women in childbirth, as documented in more or less every society through history. When goddesses gave birth in myths, they, too, had the help of other goddesses as midwives. A male magician might have been called in to administer a spell or offer some supernatural advice now and then, but the mysteries of conception and birth required women's wisdom, passed down through time.

Relief from the temple of Hathor at Dendera – a woman
squats to give birth, helped by two goddesses.

Childbirth was one of the most important events in most women's lives, and one they might experience several times. The safe birth of a child wasn't solely an individual concern but a social one, shared by the wider community. The expectant parents, their extended family, and their entire village or neighbourhood would have seen childbirth as part of the interlocking cycles of cosmic renewal, including the changing seasons of the year and the daily rebirth of the sun. The story of Isis and her son Horus was an important source of divine inspiration for pregnant women and new mothers, so much so that over time, the male-dominated world of the Egyptian temple

Paintings of marsh scenes refer to sensual pleasures and hidden dangers –
here in the tomb of an official named Menna.

started to include a dedicated mini-temple where the local goddess could magically, eternally give birth to the temple's main god. Making love and making babies is what keeps the world turning.

With every potential renewal, however, came the worry that things might go wrong. A woman might not be able to get pregnant, or to carry a pregnancy to term. Giving birth was fraught with danger for both mother and child, and even after a successful delivery, the mother's body needed to recover and an infant needed to be able to nurse, gain weight, and flourish. Small wonder that a host of magic spells, and charms, administered by wise women with the help of specialist demi-gods, existed to help ensure a successful outcome in the face of cosmic threats.

Wine, women, and song

As the old jazz standard puts it, 'I've got it bad, and that ain't good'. This love song might be the ancient Egyptian equivalent:

> For seven days until yesterday I have not seen my beloved. Illness has possessed me.
>
> My limbs have become heavy, and I have lost all control over myself.
>
> If the greatest of doctors came to me, my heart would not be satisfied with their remedies.
>
> Even the reading-priests cannot find the way. My illness is not recognized.

Even the reading-priests – those experts on magical literature – seem to have floundered in the face of lovesickness. Magic was no cure for a broken heart, but some familiar magic symbols, such as watery realms and crocodiles, make an appearance in verses of yearning like these. Sensual, even sultry, love poetry often has a rhythm in the ancient language that suggests it was set to music – and music was one way to woo a lover and 'enjoy a pleasant hour', as the Egyptians would have put it, with a knowing wink.

The pleasures of love and sex were an important part of life, even if they sometimes led to heartache and betrayal – or even baldness, if that spiteful recipe for hair loss really worked. What emerges from the ancient love songs, which are often set among lush gardens, the life-giving marshes, or drunken festivals, especially in honour of Hathor and other goddesses, is a sense of playful eroticism. The poems – 'sweet songs', as one papyrus called them – praise the beauty of young women waiting to meet their male lovers, or vice versa, since male beauty was equally celebrated. 'He offered me the charm of his loins', one young woman declares, concluding happily with the observation that 'it is longer than it is wide'.

Lovers often met on the banks of a river or canal in these poems, and one makes explicit reference to the water-spells that magically protected the couple from the animals who lurked in the waters. 'A voracious crocodile was waiting on the sandbank,' laments a young man trying to reach his girlfriend on the opposite side. Fortunately, her love is so strong that it enchants the crocodile and turns it into a mouse. Other songs were quite explicit about what would happen when the two lovers managed to meet: 'Fill her gateway,' one advised: 'It will shake, and her arbour will overflow.'

Many objects and motifs in ancient Egyptian art complement the imagery of the love songs – and provide further clues that romance wasn't the only magic at work in such couplings. Scenes painted on tomb walls during the New Kingdom show lush banquets where beautifully adorned guests drink wine while musicians and dancing girls perform. The atmosphere is intensely erotic, with incense, perfume, and flowers scenting the air. The guests and musicians wear floral wreaths, their best braids, and diaphanous clothing – or, in the case of the dancing girls, no clothing at all. Scholars have suggested that these scenes may represent religious festivals, in particular those in which drunkenness and music were meant to lure Hathor, the sun-god's daughter, back to Egypt after she has flounced off in a huff. This, or a similar, festival may have been timed with the arrival of the flood at new year, with its promise of new life. Encouraging and celebrating human fertility was a natural counterpart to this natural process.

It also looks like it was a lot of fun. Certainly the ancient Egyptians themselves made ribald jokes and satirical sketches out of such occasions. A famous, if fragmentary, papyrus roll in the collection of the Egyptian Museum in Turin has drawings of a religious festival in which animals take the place of the priests, followed by several explicit scenes that show beautiful, bored-looking young women having sex with balding, paunchy men, in absurdly acrobatic positions. There was a serious side to sexuality in a religious or magical context, though. The reason Hathor needed to return to Egypt, according to myths, was so that her health, wholeness, and beauty would encourage her father Ra to regenerate himself overnight; no less than the continued survival of the cosmos was at stake.

To us, the Turin papyrus may seem exploitative or pornographic, while the idea of a divine daughter using her beauty to entice or inspire her father is downright repugnant. But as we've seen time and again, myth and magic often operate on the edge of social taboos, or consciously subvert them. Moreover, the apparent objectification of beautiful adolescent females in art might well have appealed to women as well as men. Spoons for perfume oils with handles in the shape of nubile, nude girls were probably used by both men and women, as were small make-up vessels in the form of cheeky monkeys. The goddess Hathor – whom the Greeks equated with Aphrodite – had both male and female devotees, judging by offerings made in her honour at the temple of Deir el-Bahri on the edge of the Valley of the Kings. These included faience bowls, perhaps used for festive drinking or to leave offerings (or both), which were decorated with images such as tilapia (Nile catfish, another symbol of fertility, because of its observed behaviour of keeping its numerous young safe in its mouth), lotus flowers, or women strumming harps, reminiscent of

Wine, perfume, and lotus flowers lend a heady air
to banquet scenes in New Kingdom tombs.

A rare painting on leather combines
music with comic sexuality.

the musicians in tomb paintings of banqueting scenes. Hathor and
other goddesses, such as Isis, were also associated with a musical
instrument called the *shesheshat* after the soothing, rattling sound
it made, which has come down to us, via Latin, as a *sistrum*.

But what if you weren't having any luck in love, even with the
help of music and alcohol? There were magic spells to help a man
attract – and keep – a woman, such as this one, which calls on the
god of the evening sun and Hathor in her seven-fold form and was
said to foretell the fate of newborn babies:

Hail to you Re-Horakhty, father of the gods! Hail to you,
seven Hathors who are clothed in wrappings of red linen!
Hail to you, gods, lords of heaven and earth! Let So-and-so

[the desired woman] come after me like a cow going after
grass, like a maidservant chasing after her children, like
a herdsman looking after his cattle.

The magician concludes the spell by threatening to set fire to the
ancient Delta city of Buto if it fails, but let's hope it didn't come to that.

Thwarted love and cheating lovers never did bring out the best
in anyone. In the tales of magical exploits told to entertain King
Khufu, prince Khafre offers the story of a chief reading-priest named
Webauner who discovered that his wife had taken a lover, whom she
liked to meet near an ornamental lake in their garden. Webauner
made a wax crocodile, performed a spell over it, and gave it to one
of his gardeners to place in the lake, where it promptly came to
life and seized the lover. Webauner turned the crocodile back into
wax, and sent his straying wife to the king for punishment. Needless
to say, she was not met with much sympathy. Written by and for an
elite male audience, ancient Egyptian stories like the Khufu tales
often depicted women as scheming or unfaithful, such as the stun-
ning priestess Tabubu in the stories of Setne.

The magical texts often reflect the same male-centred concerns,
so it's no surprise to find magical-medical prescriptions designed to
inflame lust in a reluctant woman or to help a man get and maintain
an erection. As a cure for impotence, one recipe suggested grinding
acacia and *Zizyphus* leaves with honey, and applying the remedy to
the unresponsive body part with a bandage. Attempts to improve
male sexual potency were not just for recreation, but also for reproduction; the ancient Egyptians understood that male sperm was
necessary for conception. And reproduction meant rebirth in a more
mystical sense as well: a spell in the Coffin Texts promised that after
death, the deceased would be able to have sex night and day, with as
many women as he chose. A man was obviously the default setting
for such funerary magic.

Men resorted to magic to win women over in life as well. Less appealing was a spell to try to make a woman fall in love – or lust – with you. It was written down in two forms of Egyptian, with some words spelled out in unusual ways, as if the scribe were uncertain or wanted to confuse anyone who might stumble across the papyrus and try to read it. The scribe also put some key words into cryptic characters, making the meaning even more difficult to decipher; these ultra-secret words are in boldface below:

> To make a woman **crazy** [with desire] for a man. You should bring a live **shrewmouse**, remove its **gall**, and put it in one place; remove its **heart** and put it in another place. You should take its whole body and pound it carefully when it is dry. You should mix a little of the pounded remains with a little blood from your second finger and the little finger of your left hand; you should put this in a cup of wine and make the woman drink it. She is **crazy** for you.

The shrewmouse was sacred to the sun-god, which might explain its appearance in this recipe. Any woman who found out that pulverized shrewmouse and human blood had been added to her wine certainly had good reason to go crazy, but perhaps not in the way the magician and his scheming client had intended.

Attracting a specific woman was the intention of one of the most complete – and chilling – examples of ancient magical practice found in Egypt. Dating to the Roman period, the find consists of a ceramic pot that contained a clay figure and a tightly rolled sheet of lead. The clay figure represents a naked woman with carefully coifed hair, her knees bent and her arms behind her back, pinioned like a bound prisoner, while the lead sheet was incised with directions to the magician about how to make and use the figurine. The magician was to take thirteen copper needles and stick them into specific parts

A clay figure pierced with needles matches the
instructions in a curse tablet found buried with it.

of the figure's body, including the sensory organs, genitals, navel, hands, and feet, reciting each time, 'I am piercing your ears, eyes, mouth [and so on], so that So-and-so [the woman] will remember no one but me', ending each time with the name of the male client.

The result is a well-made, fired-clay figure that looks like a voodoo doll, stuck through with thirteen needles – the holes for which had to be made before the figure went into the kiln, since fired clay is too hard to pierce. In a similar way to knots made in cords or strips of papyrus, the needles fixed the magical wish to the figure's body, rather than harming the body of the actual woman the figure was meant to represent. In other words, it isn't magic meant to cause harm or pain. Nonetheless, looking at this ensemble today, it seems like a rather extreme measure for trying to win someone's love or loyalty. This is one of the ugly sides of Egyptian magic, and we can only hope that the woman in question found someone more deserving.

Baby-making

If your romance went smoothly – ideally without the need for impotence remedies, powdered mice, or figures to use as a pincushion – you and your beloved might find yourself in the family way. The sexual imagery of the love poems, banquet scenes, and decoration of more everyday objects, like cosmetic containers, all evoked the fecundity of the natural world and the fertility of human beings. While some magic clearly reflected specifically male concerns about sexual performance, on a cosmic level, it was in everyone's interest to make love – and make babies.

Having children was the norm in ancient Egyptian society, but for some people, that was easier said than done. At the village of Deir el-Medina, a couple named Ramose and Mutemwia made several devotional offerings to divinities associated with fertility and childbirth, but they never seem to have had a child of their own. Of course, there were also women who wanted or needed to avoid getting pregnant, perhaps because they could not afford another child, or because they were having sex with someone other than their husband, or as a way to earn a living. Since the ancient Egyptians understood that male ejaculation led to pregnancy, inserting something into the vagina to try to block the sperm seemed worth the attempt, if you could stomach the pessary of sour milk, honey, and 'crocodile dung' (perhaps soil of some kind). Alternatively, you might brew up a herbal contraceptive recipe; one called for celery to be smoked with grains of emmer, then mixed with beer and vegetable oil, boiled, and taken for four mornings in a row.

In addition to using contraceptives, a woman might want a test to determine whether or not she was pregnant. One magical-medical text instructed a woman to fill one bag with emmer wheat grains and another with barley. By moistening each bag with her urine every day, she would soon have an answer: if both varieties of grain sprouted, a baby was on the way. A modern doctor in England put this ancient remedy to the test in laboratory conditions, but found that there was absolutely no correlation between seed sprouting and whether or not the urine sample came from a pregnant woman.

Staying pregnant was a worry, too, judging by spells that guarded against unexpected or heavy bleeding, of the kind a woman would experience during miscarriage. One such spell combines an incantation with the knotting of a cloth, to be inserted into the vagina to staunch the flow and magically try to stop it altogether:

Anubis has come forth to keep the flood from trespassing
on what is pure: the land of Tait. Beware of what is in it.
This spell to be said over the threads on the border of a
textile, with a knot made in it. To be applied to the inside
of the vagina.

Tait was the goddess of linen, which made her an appropriate focus of a magic spell requiring linen, and Anubis may have been invoked here because of his association with the sacred linen bandages used in wrapping the mummified dead. The spell calls for a strip of linen with a fringe on one edge, meaning that it came from the end of the cloth, where some threads had been left unwoven, as was sometimes done for decorative effect. Knotting the textile served both to 'fix' the magician's words into it and to bulk up its absorbency. Heavy bleeding at the wrong time of the month was an alarming symptom at any time, but all the more so during pregnancy. The spell compares excess or ill-timed bleeding to a Nile flood that was higher than expected and thus destructive – another instance of a good, healthy, life-affirming thing, like a menstrual period, turning into a disaster, in this case a private and poignant one.

Once a pregnancy was safely established and starting to show, the inevitable questioning would start: what are you hoping for, a boy or a girl? The trusty emmer-and-barley pregnancy test promised a solution here, too. After an expectant mother had applied her urine to the bags of emmer and barley for several days, she should observe which sprouted first: if it was the barley, she would have a boy. If it was the emmer, prepare for a girl. No doubt older women in the household or community had their own opinions to share on this matter as well – predicting a baby's sex seems to be a pastime as old as the pyramids. No one would really know whether a little Ramose or a Nefret was on the way until the mother was safely delivered of a healthy child. Giving birth – whether for the first time or the fifteenth – was a pivotal moment in the life cycle of a woman, her family, and the infant whose life hung in the balance. For childbirth was also mysterious, painful, messy, and dangerous: definitely something for which you'd want every kind of magic on your side.

Magic and motherhood

Just as Isis and Horus, the archetypal mother and child, were a crucial reference point in Egyptian healing magic, so too did they provide a magical model for the safe delivery of a baby and its subsequent survival. Infant and child mortality was high (perhaps 10 to 20 per cent), as was the risk of a mother dying in childbirth, or shortly afterwards from infection. Similar patterns have been the norm in most societies around the world, and ancient Egypt was no different.

As the goddess of sexuality and fertility, Hathor was also invoked in protective magic for childbirth. In later periods of Egyptian history,

Hathor was closely linked to the dwarf-god Bes, who was an important aid to women as they laboured. This animal–human hybrid was closely linked with the protection of newborn babies, and often appeared in Horus-on-the-crocodiles motifs, usually directly above the vulnerable Horus, as on the Metternich stela. His human body had the proportions of an achondroplastic dwarf, and his face was that of a lion's, framed by a mane and contorted so that the skin creased, the eyes bulged, and the tongue protruded from an open mouth. His leonine face and exposed genitals frightened away evil spirits, and some images show him wielding a short sword or knife for the same reason. Bes was also prone to bursts of unrestrained dancing and musical performances; on his own or with the hippo-goddess Taweret, he can be depicted strumming a stringed instrument, shaking a tambourine, or banging a drum, although whether this was to frighten off spirits, celebrate the occasion, or (more pragmatically) cover the cries of the woman in labour, is difficult to say. But it was probably his human nature that invited his association with children; although it sounds like an insulting attitude to us now, in ancient Egypt a dwarf's 'childlike' physical proportions suggested that he or she was eternally youthful – they grew without growing up.

Some magic spells that aimed to ease the pain of childbirth invoked the Isis and Horus story, Hathor, and Bes (or another dwarf deity) all at the same time. One such spell instructs the magician to place a plant-based poultice on the head of the suffering woman, while reciting this spell-within-a-story several times:

I am Horus. I was thirsty, and I came down from the
mountain. I found someone calling out, weeping. His wife
was nearing her time. I got him to stop weeping. His wife
called out for an image of a dwarf, made of clay. Let someone
hurry to Hathor, the lady of Dendera, to fetch her healing
amulet, so that Hathor will make this woman give birth!

Figures of Bes flank Taweret on the arm
of a chair from an 18th Dynasty tomb.

The magician identified himself or herself with Horus, and presumably came prepared with exactly the kind of clay dwarf figure called for in the spell, as well as the ingredients for the poultice (acacia leaves, perhaps; the writing is unclear). While we tend to assume that written, recorded spells like this one were intended for use by male magicians, we know that it was women who helped other women give birth. Therefore we should be open to the possibility that some midwives also knew how to use such spells, recipes, and images in their work.

A clay figure of a dwarf also featured in a spell that seems to encourage safe delivery of the placenta:

> Come down, placenta, come down! I am Horus, the
> magician, and the woman who has given birth is already
> feeling better, as if she has finished her labour....Hathor
> will place her hand on this woman as a healing amulet.
> I am Horus, who saves her!

This spell was to be recited four times over the clay figure before setting it at or near the woman's head.

The placement of the figure near the new mother's head suggests that by that point, she was lying down and having a well-earned rest. However, a seated or squatting position was the usual position in which women delivered their babies, as we know from some rare depictions of childbirth (not to mention human biology). Stacks of bricks made of sun-baked clay may have offered support for women to squat on or lean against as they laboured. Conventionally there were four of these birth bricks, the number associated with the four cardinal directions. The bricks were collectively given divine form in the goddess Meskhenet, whose name meant 'bricks'. She is one of four goddesses who arrive at the house of Redjedet to help deliver her of triplets in one of the nested stories of magic told to entertain

King Khufu. Meskhenet sometimes appears, in the form of a brick, next to the balance scales in the judgment scene from the Book of the Dead. Birth bricks were placed in the four walls of royal burial chambers during the New Kingdom, another example of the conceptual link between the birth of a child and the rebirth of the dead.

A rare example of a decorated birth brick was excavated at the site of Abydos in southern Egypt in 2001. It was made of mud, formed in a mould and dried in the sun and each external face preserves traces of colourful decoration. The short sides of the brick were painted with protective animals and demi-gods, while its largest preserved surface depicts an elegant woman, seated on a throne with an infant on her lap. Another woman stands behind her, and a third kneels in front of the throne. Each woman has blue hair. Blue was a special pigment both because it had to be created artificially (as opposed to organic white, black, red, and yellow) and because of its divine symbolism. Gods and goddesses were said to have hair made of lapis lazuli; therefore, colouring the hair of the female figures in blue suggests that they are meant to represent women of divine status. The emblems that frame the scene bear the cow-faces of the goddess Hathor, giving a further clue to the imagery evoked on this otherwise modest-looking object. Some of the protective figures on the sides

Mud brick painted with birth scenes –
and perhaps used by women in childbirth.

of the brick have blue hair or bodies, too, including a lion-faced female holding snakes, who resembles the wooden figure found in the Ramesseum magician's grave.

Scholars have suggested several options for how these bricks might have been used, whether for women to squat or lean on during the delivery, or to help define a zone of protection around the labouring woman. Bricks could also be lined up to form a protective platform on which to place the newborn baby. Any or all of these are possible. Women seem to have retreated to a space set apart for birth, whether in their own household or somewhere nearby, and may have stayed apart from the normal routines of the community for several days or even weeks while recovering from the birth and nursing the infant. Many of the practices around birth will have depended on the social status of the mother and her family, of course. At Deir el-Medina, a village that housed the skilled artists who decorated the royal tombs in the Valley of the Kings, several houses have elevated platforms in the front room, decorated with images of Bes and young female musicians. Some scholars have suggested that these offered a space for lovemaking and childbirth, but they may simply have served as places for prayers and offerings aimed at ensuring the health and wellbeing of the entire household.

Another suggestion is that an outdoor structure of some kind sheltered labouring women and new mothers. The idea of a birth arbour or bower comes from depictions of nursing women surrounded by vine-like plants and sitting under some kind of pergola, although whether such images should be taken to represent real spaces, or symbolic ones, is difficult to say. The vines may be birthwort, *Aristolochia clematitis*, a twining plant with heart-shaped leaves, the juice of which has been used in some cultures to induce labour, encourage sleep, and support the functioning of the womb. A coffin made for a woman named Isis, whose mummy does not survive, represents her in a splendid white robe holding stems of birthwort in her hands, inviting the question of whether she might have died in childbirth. The same plant may decorate the shrine or bower in which a statue of a princess named Meketaten is shown in a tomb for the royal family at the city of Amarna; the tomb scene depicts her funeral rites, which seem to allude to her having died after delivering a grandchild for King Akhenaten and Queen Nefertiti.

Regardless of where a woman gave birth, there was a time-honoured magical tool to protect her and her child: a wand made of hippopotamus ivory and incised with protective spirits and demi-gods, and sometimes the names of the mother and child. These birth tusks, as they have recently been termed, have usually been found in burials – including the Ramesseum magician's tomb – but they were clearly used in life. Many have been repaired after a break, or show signs of wear and re-working along their sides and especially at their pointed ends. These well-rubbed ends may have been used to mark out a protective circle for any number of magic rites, especially those related to childbirth and children – the tusks are often

Birth tusk, made of hippopotamus ivory
and incised with magical figures.

associated in tomb scenes or burials with women identified as caring for children. We can easily imagine that such tusks were a valued part of a magician or midwife's equipment.

The images incised onto the birth tusks were not for decorative purposes, but magic ones. They include animal figures from the magical menagerie, such as lions, baboons, and a lion-hippo hybrid, plus frogs, turtles, and a fantastic winged wildcat with a falcon's head. Human figures with animal heads make an appearance too, notably the Bes-like figure sometimes named as Aha, and a similar figure with female breasts, usually grasping snakes in either hand and, therefore, more or less identical to the blue-painted figure on the edges of the Abydos birth brick. The similarity of such images, and the way they echo the forms and symbolism of other figures of similar date, suggests a coherent cosmic realm of protective forces on which magicians could call in the centuries around 2000 to 1500 BCE. And although much of this symbolism is connected to childbirth, we should not imagine that this restricted it to birthing events or to stereotypically 'female' concerns. Protection against harm was something everyone needed – starting with the smallest, and newest, members of the community.

The mouths of babes

Magical protection didn't stop with the moment of birth. Newborn infants are entirely helpless, and if something had gone wrong during the pregnancy or birth, for instance malnourishment or the death of the mother, the risk to the newborn was considerable. Baby's first amulet could be made as follows:

'Are you warm in the nest? Are you hot among the
bushes? Is your mother not with you? Is there no sister
to offer a breeze? Is there no nurse for protection?

Let there be brought to me beads of gold, beads of carnelian, a sealing-bead with a crocodile on it, and a hand-pendant(?) to slay and to dispel the female demon *Mereret*, to warm the body, to slay the male and female enemies in the West. You will break free!' This is a protection [*sa*]. To be said over beads of gold and carnelian, a sealing-bead with a crocodile, and a hand-pendant. To be strung on a strip of fine linen, to be made into an amulet and applied to the throat of a child. Good.

What the spell instructs the magician to make sounds like a rather pretty beaded necklace, but this was not merely jewelry. Each bead had a particular magical meaning, giving the necklace the power to ward off any demonic threats to the child.

A mother's own milk was the best and most obvious choice of nutrition for a newborn. Ancient Egyptian women were probably also aware that nursing could be a form of contraception, since it delays the return of ovulation in some women. The use of wet nurses seems to have been an established practice, whether because the mother had died, because she didn't produce enough milk, or perhaps for reasons of preference or social status. Wet nurses themselves could be women of high status: several tombs honour women who had been royal wet nurses, or a high-status man might honour his wet nurse in his own tomb, as if she had become part of the family. A tiny faience feeding cup found in the village of Lisht in the Fayum has a spout small enough to drip milk or liquified food into an infant's mouth. Depicted around the outside of the cup are protective figures similar to those incised on the birth tusks, as if imbuing the milk offered to the child with additional, magical nourishment. If the cup were used for an ailing infant, perhaps one whose own mother couldn't feed him or her, there is an added poignancy and precariousness to the nourishment that child needed in order to survive.

Already at the moment of birth, the midwife's action of clearing mucus from a baby's mouth may have inspired the Opening of the Mouth ritual that *sem*-priests performed on newly-made statues and on wrapped mummies to make them fully alive and sentient. During this rite, the priest touched the mouth of the statue or wrapped mummy with an instrument known as the *netjery* ('divine') tool, in the shape of two small fingers – all that would fit into the mouth of an infant. The need to separate the infant from its mother's body meant cutting the umbilical cord became part of the ritual as well. To do this, the midwife used a flint tool with a split blade at one end; its bifurcated shape was ideal for cutting through a tube or cord. This tool, called the *peshes-kef*, became part of the ceremonial equipment for Opening the Mouth. The priest also presented the statue, or wrapped mummy, with two jars called the breasts of Isis and Horus, which represent the nourishment of breast-feeding. Through these ritual gestures and recitations, the private act of giving birth was transformed into the cosmic act of being reborn after death, which connected pregnancy and motherhood to one of the greatest supernatural concerns that ran throughout Egyptian society.

Feeding cup in faience, circled with
protective knives and animals.

By the Late Period (*c.* 600 BCE), the cosmic connections of giving birth began to play a more prominent role in Egyptian mythology and temple ritual. The main god or goddess worshipped in a temple became part of a family group consisting of mother, father, and divine child. Every divine mother needed a safe place for labour and delivery, and as a result, shrines or small temples dedicated to childbirth began to be built. Known in Egyptology as *mammisi* (from a Coptic Egyptian phrase meaning 'place of birth'), these birth temples were usually located just in front of the gateway to the main temple. The decoration of the birth temples included Bes, often with musical instruments, and goddesses to assist at the delivery. The main focus of the decoration was after the birth, when the divine child was breastfed by his mother and placed on his throne. Like Horus, every newly born deity was male and destined to be king. Birth temples could be seen as examples of what happens when high-status men take over an otherwise female domain, like childbirth, and turn it to their ends. Still, the goddess who gave birth to the divine child was there to protect and nourish him, as Isis had done for Horus – and as the Virgin Mary would do for Jesus not long afterwards, when early Christians turned to ideas of holy pregnancy and divine birth for their own supernatural superstar.

Opposite Miniature column with Hathor-emblems,
the same form favoured at temple birth-houses.

PREDICTING THE FUTURE

Given how many things could go wrong in life in ancient Egypt, it's no surprise that people looked for ways to try to predict or influence the future by supernatural means. Egyptian society valued order and predictability, summed up in the concept of *maat* – cosmic justice – and epitomized by the annual return of the Nile flood. But like the level of the flood waters, which priests monitored at measuring points known today as Nilometers, life did not always yield what you had hoped. If magic could give a hint at what was to come, or deliver divine advice, why not accept a helping hand from higher powers?

All magic tried to create an optimal outcome for the user, whether that meant flourishing crops, a healthy child, or a faithful lover. Predictive magical practices tried to stop a problem from arising in the first place, whether by seeking supernatural advice or identifying the most auspicious time to take a certain course of action. As we'll see in this chapter, some predictions took place in a public forum. In small, close-knit communities, individual choices could have an impact on everyone, after all – and the priests who organized public predictions were undoubtedly aware of the potential ramifications. Other methods of predicting the future, or interpreting the gods' advice, took place in private forms of consultation, where the role of the magical expert was to guide the inner reflections of the client.

Although we find no direct equivalent in Egypt for the ancient Greek concept of fate (embodied in the Greek goddess Nemesis), there was nonetheless an element of fatalism in ancient Egyptian thought. Living was tough and death was the only thing waiting at the end.

No wonder it could seem as if the gods had it in for humankind, as if the course of life had been predetermined, set on a path entirely out of our control. Birth magic alluded to this idea in the form of the Seven Hathors, avatars of the goddess that were said to attend the birth of a baby and decide its fate. Yet the incredible array of magical practices in ancient Egypt make it clear that people hoped to have a hand in their own fate, too, even if the odds sometimes seemed stacked against them. When she was in a good mood, Hathor herself would certainly have agreed that hope springs eternal – and what could be more magical than that.

All you have to do is dream

The ancient Egyptians saw sleep as a stage of consciousness in which meeting with a ghost or god, usually bearing a positive or helpful message from beyond, was possible. As a prince, the future pharaoh Thutmose IV fell asleep at midday in the shadow of the Sphinx at Giza, and dreamed the sphinx itself – embodiment of the god Horemakhet – asked him to clear away the sand that had drifted over it. This he did, and erected a 3.6-metre (12-foot) high stela between the paws of the Sphinx to record the episode.

But you didn't need to be royal to receive messages in your sleep. At the village of Deir el-Medina, a scribe named Qenherkhepeshef owned a library of papyri that passed to his wife and her family after he died, during the reign of Ramses II (c. 1280–1210 BCE). Among them is the earliest known manual for the interpretation of dreams, which its owner might have used only for himself or to give advice to others. Dreams are always described as acts of sight, as if the sleeping person is having a vision, and symbols in dreams are treated as omens of what might come. The manual lists dreams in neat rows, using a formula that runs like this:

> If a man sees himself in a dream, drinking wine, good,
> it means living according to *maat*.

> If a man sees himself in a dream, seeing a crane, good,
> it means prosperity.

> If a man sees himself in a dream, seeing a large tomcat,
> good, it means a large harvest will come.

For these dreams that give good omens, the link between what the dreamer sees and what it means is sometimes rather general (wine-drinking – positive!) and often based on wordplay. For instance, the Egyptian word for a crane, *dja*, echoed the sound of *wedja*, meaning prosperity. The 'large tomcat' in the last example may be the mythical cat that kills the evil serpent Apep, ensuring the renewal of the sun and life itself – including, logically, a good harvest.

Dreams that delivered bad news worked on similar principles, often alluding to social norms that became negative only in the context of the dream:

> If a man sees himself in a dream, having sex with his wife
> during the day, bad, it means his god will see his crimes.

> If a man sees himself in a dream, writing on a papyrus
> scroll, bad, it means his god will judge his crimes.

In the first example, it isn't that making love by day was necessarily bad, but that it created the possibility of being caught in the act, just as the gods might catch out wrong-doing. Likewise, the act of writing was ordinarily very positive in ancient Egypt, but here, a dream about writing seems to evoke the judgment of the dead, where the god of writing, Thoth, recorded the outcome of the divine tribunal.

Wooden headrest incised with an image
of Bes to protect the sleeper.

In addition to the divination of dreams, there were several magical measures sleepers could take to encourage good dreams and guard against nightmares. Spells against nightmares called for four clay cobras with fire in their mouths – possibly oil lamps – to be placed in the corners of the sleeping room (see Chapter 4). Sleeping on a headrest decorated with protective images, such as Bes figures, also helped ensure sweet dreams and an uninterrupted night.

Using dreams to predict the future or seek advice was a practice that continued into Roman times, with several dream manuals written in the Demotic Egyptian language and script that was used in later periods of Egyptian history. Magic could help someone invite a god to visit them in their dreams, as this spell explains:

O Isis, O Nephthys, O noble spirit of Osiris Wennefer, come to me, because I am your beloved son Horus. O gods who are in the sky, O gods who are on the earth, O gods who are in the primeval ocean, O gods who are in the south, O gods who are in the north, O gods who are in the west, O gods who are in the east, come to me in this night, instruct me about such-and-such a matter, about which I am enquiring. Quickly, quickly, hurry, hurry.

Words to be said over a *benu*-bird drawn with myrrh water, juice of *any*-wood, and black ink on your right hand and recite these writings to it in the evening, while your hand is outstretched opposite the moon. When you go to sleep, you put your hand under your head. Good, good, four times.

The title for this spells calls it a *peh-netjer*, or oracle, of Osiris, the idea being that it granted the sleeping person the chance to consult Osiris directly through the magically induced dream.

Another way to solicit a message from the gods is known by scholars as incubation, although this kind of incubation had nothing to do with hatching eggs. It refers to the practice of sleeping inside the accessible spaces of a temple, or in rooms specially designed for the purpose, in hopes that the god or goddess of the temple would appear in a dream. It isn't clear if this practice was available to everyone equally, or if it required certain payments, preparations, or social status. In Roman Egypt, large temples had special sanctuaries set aside as sleeping quarters, and priests were probably on hand the next morning to help interpret what you had seen. The advice of a priest or magician was often necessary to decipher what the gods were trying to tell you; dream manuals seem to collect such advice for consultation either inside or outside the temple. If you could extract the messages from your dream, you might adjust your daily schedule according to what they advised, or shape longer-term plans to heed whatever warning, or encouragement, the dream had offered.

Timing it right

Another way to decide a propitious, or inauspicious, time for any activity you might want to undertake was to consult a calendar of good and bad days. These calendars probably originate in the temple sphere, where priests followed restrictions on certain festival days, but they seem to have circulated more widely too. The calendars use black ink to indicate good days and red ink for bad ones. Ignore the warnings and suffer death by crocodile. Some of the ventures warned against on specific days were building a house, setting off on a journey, or having sex. Many calendars prohibit particular foods or drink on certain days, another indication that these calendars might reflect priestly regimens. Day three of the first month of Akhet, at the start of the year, was a lucky day as long as you didn't eat fish, while the next day was unlucky for anyone with heart trouble, who was sure to drop dead.

The worst possible time to start any new venture was during the demon days that fell at the end of the 360-day solar year and before the start of the flood season, normally in mid- or late July. As we have seen, these five 'extra' days, separating one year from the next, were dangerous times, requiring special amulets to protect against the violent forces sent out by an angry Sekhmet. A papyrus now in Leiden includes a spectacular spell to try, with the recitation first and the instructions afterwards:

Hail to you gods, murderers who stand in waiting upon
Sekhmet, who have come forth from the Eye of Ra,
messengers in every district who cause the slaughter, who
create uproar, who race through the land, who shoot arrows
from their mouths, who can see from afar! Be on your way,
be distant from me. I shall not go with you. You shall have
no power over me. You shall not throw your net over me, to
catch me for the slaughter. You shall not cause me any bad

luck this year, for I am Ra, who appears in his Eye. I have arisen as Sekhmet, I have arisen as Wadjet [the cobra-goddess]. I am Atum in the temple, the lord of mankind, who made the gods. I am the Powerful One, lofty and high!

Words to be said over a piece of fine linen. These gods are to be drawn on it, and it is to be knotted twelve times. Offer them bread, beer, and burning incense. Apply the amulet to a man's throat. A means to save a man from the plague of the year; an enemy will have no power over him. A means to placate the gods in the retinue of Sekhmet and Thoth. Words to be said from the last day of the year to the first day of the new year.

The violent imagery of the spell brings the threat of the demon days vividly to life, countered by the magician who speaks in the voice of the gods – first Ra, then his daughters or 'Eyes', Sekhmet and Wadjet, and finally Atum, a creator-god of such potency and mystery that he was simply known as 'the Powerful One'.

What a relief it must have been when New Year's Day finally dawned. Festivals in every town and temple greeted the start of the new year, when all the demons were banished (at least for a little while). Special flasks holding sacred water were distributed at these events during the Late Period (c. 650–400 BCE). Made of pale-green faience, the flasks had to be formed and fired well before the festivals took place. Many are decorated with images of papyrus plants from the Nile marshes and floral wreaths around their necks. Hieroglyphic inscriptions wish the recipient of the flask a happy new year, or in Egyptian, *wep-renpet nefer*, literally, a good, beautiful, or perfect (*nefer*) repeating-of-the-year. We don't know if the water inside the flasks was water that had been through some magical transformation, like the water poured over healing statues and Horus-on-the-crocodiles

New Year's flask made of faience, inscribed
for a priest named Amenhotep, son of Iufaa.

images. It's a possibility, though, and the flasks demonstrate the close connections that temples created between priests, rituals, and the rhythms of everyday life.

The voice of god

Dream manuals and the almanac-like calendars of lucky and unlucky days reveal how Egyptians tried to chart their course in life by optimizing what the future had in store for them. Thanks to the connections that existed between temples and their local communities, however, there was a more direct and public way to consult the gods as well. Egyptian oracles were very different from the oracles of the ancient Greek world, which could be contacted only at certain places (famously Delphi), via the person, often a woman, who served as the god's mouthpiece. In contrast, in ancient Egypt consulting an oracle was a public affair that took place during festivals, when a processional statue of the local god or goddess was carried out of the temple and paraded through the streets, held aloft by priests. The Egyptians referred to these festivals as *peh-netjer*, meaning 'the god's arrival', because they were among the rare occasions when people other than priests found themselves in the presence of a divine image – even if that image was shrouded and partly concealed inside a shrine, high up on the model boat in which it 'sailed' through the crowds.

Procession oracles worked by writing yes-or-no questions on pieces of papyrus or potsherds and leaving them in the path of the procession. The god steered its boat towards the correct answer, as the divine power magically moved the priests in one direction.

Opposite Unfinished stela of Amennakht,
showing a sacred boat procession used as an oracle.

(This worked especially well if the questions had been submitted to the temple ahead of time.) The opinion expressed by the god had the weight of a legal decision: 'Is it So-and-so who has stolen this mat?' might declare someone's guilt or innocence. The gods were also asked for their advice on business matters: 'Is this calf good so that I may accept it?' Consulting the oracle was taken seriously – records from the reign of Ramses IX (*c.* 1125 BCE) show that a workman was granted time off to go and file a petition, perhaps in advance of a procession. In the 7th century BCE, fifty priests witnessed an oracle of Amun-Ra at Karnak in Thebes, after one of their members consulted the god for permission to transfer to the priesthood of a nearby temple in honour of the god Montu. Amun-Ra did grant his permission, and this momentous event was recorded on a papyrus more than 5 metres (16 feet) long, signed by each of the priests who witnessed it.

Oracles worked by magic, of course. Specifically, they worked by the force of *heka* that animated the gods and, thus, the priests and processions that conveyed their wishes. As the divine embodiment of magic, the god Heka was known as the 'lord of oracles and lord of revelations, who predicts what will happen', and his name could be written so that it looked like the expression for an oracle, *peh-netjer*. But oracles clearly played an important social role, as well as their divine one. The public forum in which they took place must have allowed the local priesthood to resolve local disputes and ease tensions, or conversely draw attention to unethical or illegal behaviour that was otherwise without redress. This put considerable power into the priests' hands, and there must have been times when the movement of the oracle was picked over and debated like a close election result. Pride and property were often at stake.

In later periods of Egyptian history, when Egypt was embedded in the wider Mediterranean culture of Greece and Rome, priests and magicians developed further methods for soliciting a god's opinion or forecasting the future. Not only could someone sleep in the temple and hope to see (and hear) the god in a dream, but magicians also began to use young boys as mediums to channel the words of a god directly. Magic manuals written in Demotic instruct the magician to have the child stare into an oil lamp, presumably to mesmerize him, or to stand facing the rising sun at dawn, with a similarly blinding effect. It was the magician's role to interpret whatever messages the poor boy had to deliver. Magicians delved into divination by drawing lots as well: the client would toss a numbered die or chose numbered tickets, which the magician had to interpret; some numbered systems involved complex calculations, which no doubt ensured the result seemed especially mystical and reliable. Divination manuals dating to the early Roman era, written in Demotic, explained what certain numbers meant, sometimes offering encouragement to the diviner: 'Be patient! This omen is hard at first, but in the end, it is good.' Like the dream manual of Qenherkhepeshef, lists of omens collected formulaic observations that might also have been used in lot divination, or in everyday life. One example, from a village in the Fayum in the 1st or 2nd centuries CE, offered interpretations of animal behaviours to make predictions about business prospects, family life, or health. If a mouse touched a pregnant woman and it jumped away, she should beware the risk of miscarriage. Cows, donkeys, horses, scorpions, owls, and ants could all act as omens, but fate was never fixed in these manuals. Praying to the gods always offered a way to alter your destiny.

By the time Herodotus visited Egypt in the 5th century BCE, some of the oracle rituals reminded the Greek visitor of the oracles he knew from his own culture. It seems that at some Egyptian temples, specific shrines or parts of temples had become places to consult the gods and receive an answer to requests. A priest conveyed the answers to the petitioner, but the words were said to come directly from the gods. Sometimes a ticket system was in operation, whereby petitioners submitted their question in written form on two pieces of papyrus, one expecting a 'yes' answer and the other a 'no'. Whichever ticket came back to you gave you the answer.

Scholars debate whether small, concealed chambers in some temples allowed a priest to be the voice of a divine image, creating a talking statue that worked a little bit like the Great and Powerful Wizard of Oz. Though we might view such a practice with some cynicism, if both the petitioner and the priest believed that the gods moved in mysterious, magical ways, there was no reason for this not to be a perfectly serviceable way to communicate with the divine. During the Roman period, an oracle of the dwarf-god Bes at Abydos was believed to speak to visitors. This ancient city was believed to be a gateway between this world and the next, which made it a particularly potent spot. The city was sacred to Osiris, and the desert cemeteries included the tombs of the first kings of Egypt and a vast temple built by King Sety I (c. 1290 BCE), which is where the Bes oracle took place. As late as the 4th century CE, petitioners sent letters to Bes or came in person, from all over the eastern Mediterranean to seek his guidance. Pilgrims who slept in the temple's incubation chambers might receive a message from Bes in the night by following the instructions in this spell:

> Request for a dream oracle of Bes: On your left hand, draw Bes. Wrap your hand in a dark cloth of Isis and go to sleep without speaking to anyone. Wrap the rest of the cloth around your neck. Keep a small table near you so that you can write down what he says, lest you forget it after going to sleep. Sleep on a reed mat, with an unbaked brick near your head.

The papyrus included a sketch of Bes to copy, and even a recommended recipe for making the ink. Some contemporary writers looked down on Bes and other oracles as superstitious. Even worse, there were worries that Egyptian oracles were potentially subversive elements against the rule of the Roman emperor; in fact, Constantius II ordered the closure of the Bes oracle in the year 359 CE. Even so, archaeological evidence and written sources indicate that the Bes oracle at Abydos was welcoming pilgrims a hundred years later.

Starry, starry night

Egyptian priests were keen observers of the night sky, using their knowledge of astronomy to plot out monthly and annual cycles of religious ritual, culminating in the new year marked by the rise of the river's floodwaters. The alignment of the moon and stars was perceived as significant, and from as early as the Middle Kingdom there were priests who specialized in observing the movements of the heavenly bodies by night, perhaps from the rooftops of temple buildings. The moon, individual stars, and constellations of stars were associated with Egyptian deities and woven into myths and magical imagery: Thoth, the ibis-headed moon-god of writing and knowledge, the hippo-hybrid goddess associated with Ursa Major, and the dog-star Sirius (*Sopdu*, in Egyptian), which was identified with Isis, the Great Lady of Magic herself.

These hour-priests, as they were known, used their observations of the stars and knowledge of mythology to judge which days of a month or year were likely to bring good or ill fortune – the likely origin of the calendars of good and bad days. The rising and setting of constellations known as decans (because they were visible for ten nights) was linked to the mummification process, which lasted exactly as long as the seventy days required for the decans to reappear after their trip to the Duat. Observing the stars also led the ancient Egyptians to divide the night into twelve hours, which were sometimes represented as demi-goddesses with stars on their heads along the

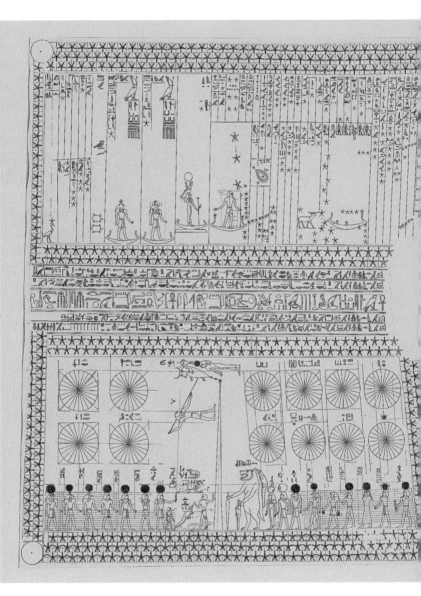

inside of a coffin lid. The interior of coffins and the ceilings of burial chambers were two of the first places where representations of the night sky appeared in Egyptian art, along with the five planets visible with the naked eye: Jupiter, Saturn, Mars, Mercury, and Venus. Most of the planets were identified with forms of the god Horus. Mercury was sometimes identified with Seth, and Venus, 'The Crosser', could be depicted as a heron. Depicting the stars and planets on the ceiling of a tomb was a display of sacred knowledge, as well as connecting the deceased to the cosmos that he (and it was usually a he) was about to join.

The ancient Egyptians clearly had a good grasp of astronomy and were interested in using it to inform day-to-day decisions. But they did not develop a form of astrology, that is, reading the position of the stars and planets at the moment of a person's birth in order to gauge their character and life-course. The twelve signs of the zodiac that we know today grew out of astronomical observations and astrological ideas in ancient Babylonia (modern Iraq). From Babylonia, knowledge of astrology began to circulate in the Greek-speaking world, which, from around 400 BCE onwards, included Egypt. Astrology may have found a ready audience in Ptolemaic and Roman Egypt, given the ancient relationship between the night sky and Egyptian myth and magic. Casting horoscopes must have seemed like a logical next step, or at least a welcome novelty. The earliest horoscope found from Egypt dates to 37 BCE and was written in Demotic, as was typical at the time.

But Egyptian magicians may already have realized the potential of using the planets to predict someone's future. A man named Harkhebi, who was both a scorpion-charmer and an hour-priest in the Delta city

Opposite Drawing of the night sky, from the ceiling of the tomb of Senenmut.

177

of Buto, is known from a statue that was set up in his honour in the 2nd century BCE. In the statue's hieroglyphic inscriptions, Harkhebi presented his many accomplishments, which include his expertise in identifying snakes and healing snake-bites – and his ability to read the omens of the sun and the dog-star Sirius. It wasn't astrology *per se*, but it does suggest that Egyptian thought was leaning that way. By the first or second century CE, a bilingual Greek and Demotic magic handbook did include instructions for casting a horoscope, which the scribe seems to have translated from Greek into Demotic as best he could. To top it off, he attributed the horoscope method to no less than Imhotep, the famous sage who had lived some three thousand years earlier. Hey presto, astrology had an Egyptian lineage.

The Egyptian priesthoods also embraced the zodiac with enthusiasm. A chapel at the temple of Hathor at Dendera had an elaborate ceiling of carved sandstone that showed the sky as a disc, held up at each corner by four goddesses and pairs of falcon-headed spirits. Thirty-six decan constellations surround the edge of the circle, equalling 360 days of the year, and the twelve signs of the zodiac are visible inside it as well, many in the familiar forms they take today: a scorpion for Scorpio, a crab for Cancer, a lion for Leo, a bull for Taurus, and the balance scales for Libra. Several other constellations adorn the sky, including our old friend the hippo-goddess, with a crocodile on her back.

In fact, the entire composition within the circle offers a map of the night sky at a specific point of time, which scholars can pinpoint to between 15 June and 15 August of the year 50 BCE. Included among the imagery are representations of a lunar eclipse (shown as an Eye of Horus) that took place on 25 September 52 BCE, and a solar eclipse (Isis holding the baboon of Thoth) known to have occurred on 7 March 51 BCE. These events must have been important enough in the life-cycle of the temple to merit recording them, along with the zodiac signs, in one of the rooftop chapels, perhaps right next

Early 19th-century engraving of the circular zodiac on the ceiling
of the temple of Hathor, Dendera – now in the Louvre.

to the roof space where such astronomical observations took place. The particular alignment of the stars in the summer of 50 BCE must also have been propitious to warrant its commemoration.

At the start of the 19th century, the zodiac of Dendera became famous in Europe thanks to drawings that were made by the French artist and diplomat Vivant Denon. Denon was among the artists and engineers brought to Egypt by Napoleon when he invaded the country in 1798, and although Napoleon's troops were eventually defeated by the British, the work of Denon and other scholars lay the groundwork for a new European encounter with Egypt. Engraved and printed in Denon's popular travel memoir, his drawings of the zodiac inspired theories about its age, its possible astrological meaning, and its religious significance. In 1821, a French engineer sawed and dynamited the zodiac out of the temple ceiling in Egypt and shipped it to Paris, where it entered the Royal Library and was later removed to the Louvre museum. That, alas, was a future that no Egyptian priest had ever foreseen.

8

MAGICAL THINKING

The fate of the Dendera zodiac was not the first instance of Europeans interfering with ancient Egypt's sacred knowledge. Roman emperors had already tried to ban Egyptian temples from the city of Rome, restrict the privileges of priest-magicians in Egypt, and, in early Christian times, stamp out the Bes oracle at Abydos. The high esteem in which Egyptian magic has been held, from ancient times to the present day, has always been both a blessing and a curse.

Many of the magic spells in this book were written down in the last few centuries of Egyptian history, that is, before the rise first of Christianity (from the 3rd century CE) and then Islam (from the 7th century CE). From around 350 BCE, not long before its conquest by Alexander the Great, Egypt was part of a well-connected, pre-dominantly Greek-speaking world that encompassed the eastern Mediterranean, North Africa, and much of modern-day Turkey and the Middle East. Egypt was a multicultural, multilingual society, which had an impact on how magic was practised, as well as the social status of magicians and priests. It also influenced how Egyptian magicians were remembered in medieval, early modern, and modern times, both in the Arab-speaking world and in Western Europe.

This final chapter considers some of the changes in Egyptian magic that took place in Roman and early Christian times and how, from there, ideas of Egyptian magical prowess and secret wisdom took hold in Europe. In the wake of the French invasion of Egypt in 1798, which targeted the country for colonization, the study of ancient Egypt gradually developed into the academic field of Egyptology.

Egyptology by and large rejected esoteric engagements with ancient Egypt, but in the late 19th and 20th centuries, many people embraced the opportunity to keep Egyptian magic, as they saw it, alive. This continues to be true today, from Kemetic churches that worship the ancient gods to theories about astrology and pyramid power, to the use of Egyptian symbols as personal talismans or commercial trademarks. The mystique of magic floats many people's boats. Perhaps Ra and Thoth, Isis and Horus, and wise old Imhotep are all happy to go along for the ride.

Bald truths

From the 4th century BCE onwards, as Egypt became more closely connected to its Eastern Mediterranean neighbours, the worship of Egyptian gods began to spread beyond Egypt, first to Greek islands and later to the Italian peninsula. And wherever the Egyptian gods went, Egyptian priests – and their magic – went with them. Before long, temples dedicated to Isis, the Great Lady of Magic herself, could be found right across the Roman world. A painting from the town of Herculaneum, near Naples, which was buried by the eruption of Mount Vesuvius in 79 CE, depicts some of the Egyptian priests who served at her temple there. They are easily recognizable by their stereotypical appearance: they wear the long white garments and shaved heads that had symbolized the personal purity required for Egyptian temple service for millennia.

Some Roman authors twisted those bald pates into a source of mockery, in stories and novels where an Egyptian priest or magician was exposed as a fool or trickster. Roman writers had a vested interest in making Egypt seem stranger or less civilized that Rome, in part to justify Rome's annexation of Egypt and to define such supposed Roman virtues as order, plain living, and civic or military virtue. This

Wall painting of Egyptian priests at a Roman Isis temple, from the town of Herculaneum, Italy.

doesn't seem to have ruffled the feathers of the ibises that strolled the grounds of all the Isis temples in Italy. And there were plenty of authors, especially those writing in Greek (rather than Latin), who admired Egypt and wrote positive accounts of the country's long traditions of learning, wisdom, and, indeed, magic. Some of the tales of Setne may have been translated into Greek, in fact, since a similar character, named Kalasiris, features in a novel by the Greek writer Heliodoros, perhaps written in the 3rd century CE. Like any Egyptian priest-magician worthy of the title, Kalasiris has secret knowledge in spades, but he plays his cards close to his chest.

In Egypt itself during the Roman era, priests and magicians were no laughing matter. They were in many ways the last bastions of the country's most ancient traditions, including its language. The last surviving hieroglyphic and Demotic inscriptions were composed by priests of Isis on the island of Philae in the 4th and 5th centuries CE respectively. At Philae, as well as the temple of Horus at Edfu around this time, it seems that a sacred falcon was kept in a large cage over the temple gateways, suggesting that animal magic still had an appeal. But the influence of Rome saw many changes occur in Egyptian society, which inevitably affected the roles played by temples and priests. For one thing, changes in taxation meant that temples, which had often enjoyed exemption under the pharaohs, lost much of their economic power. For another, there was a degree of competition from newfangled faiths, such as Mithraism and Christianity.

By the 4th century CE, the old Egyptian gods and their magic ways belonged to a shrinking circle of specialists. Places of worship were abandoned for lack of money, or lack of interest, and some priest-magicians took to the road, itinerant sorcerers who offered their services where they were wanted. Like the reading-priests and scorpion-charmers of old, these travelling magicians could offer amulets, healing spells, and words of wisdom, but in contrast to the traditional mode of worship, where gods and goddesses inhabited fortress-like temples, served by fleets of priests, magic now offered access to portable divinity.

This may be one reason for the increased use of magic gems. Carved in hard, semi-precious stones like jasper, carnelian, and amethyst, whose colours were integral to their power, these gems were used in combination with a recited spell to invoke the presence of a deity, imbuing the gem with the same power as a full-size statue. The gems were incised with imagery similar to that drawn on or described in papyrus manuals of magic, such as scorpions, crocodiles, and a snake swallowing its own tail. But new images appeared as well, in particular a rooster-headed figure with an armour-clad torso and snakes for legs. This figure is sometimes known as Abraxas, after the series of Greek letters often carved on the same gem. These letters were typical of the so-called 'magic characters' used at this time, which

Magic gem carved from jasper, showing Serapis (a Greek form of Osiris), a scorpion, a crocodile under the god's feet, and a mummy on a lion-headed bed.

look like gibberish but could be pronounced by a trained magician to cast a powerful spell. Magic characters were sometimes written in geometric shapes or spirals, too, creating visual puzzles in which letters were added or dropped for effect. If Abraxas seems to ring a bell, you might be experiencing *déjà vu* from your previous life as an ancient magician. Or you might just recognize it from the magical incantation it eventually inspired: *Abracadabra*.

Secrets and sighs

The same Greek and Egyptian milieu that gave us 'Abracadabra' yielded yet another permutation of the wise priest, a man so gifted with magic and secret knowledge that he was nearly divine: Hermes the Three-Times-Great, or Hermes Trismegistos in Greek. This Hermes was a human version of the Egyptian god Thoth, and was credited as the author of magic manuals and wisdom books that originated in Egypt and circulated throughout the Mediterranean during the Christian era. Hermes Trismegistos had a tremendous influence on medieval and early modern beliefs that Egypt was the home of magic, both in Europe and in Arabic-speaking North Africa and the Middle East. Thanks to Arabic interest in his (attributed) writings, Hermes Trismegistos was famous from southern Spain to Central Asia. As a wise man with no particular religious identity, his wisdom appealed to people of many faiths. In Christian Europe, Hermes the Three-Times-Great was thought to be a contemporary of that other great magician, Moses. He is depicted in the impressive 15th-century stone floor of Siena Cathedral, bringing his wisdom to the ancient Egyptian people, wearing attire inspired by Renaissance interpretations of Byzantine art.

One of the great feats of magic that Hermes Trismegistos was thought to have mastered was alchemy, the mystical trick of turning

Stone pavement in the cathedral of Siena, 1488:
Hermes Trismegistos brings wisdom to Egypt.

base metals into gold. Alchemy – the word itself comes from the Arabic for 'in the Egyptian manner' – was a serious intellectual and academic pursuit for centuries. The great Isaac Newton, founding member of the Royal Society in London, was an ardent alchemist. In 17th-century England, his alchemical experiments were just as much a part of 'natural philosophy' (as scientific research was then known) as his studies of force and motion. Alchemy was part of the tradition of European thought that informed the 18th-century Enlightenment, although it was later rejected as overly esoteric.

Part of a philosophical tradition known as Hermeticism, or Gnosticism, alchemy was not just the search for a key to material transformation, but a path to spiritual transformation. As such, it was embraced by self-styled secret societies, including the Rosicrucians and, to some extent, the Freemasons, both of whom are still active today and both of whom have used ancient Egyptian symbols in the construction of their identity. The Ancient Mystical Order Rosae Crucis (a branch of Rosicrucianism) has its headquarters in San Jose, California, in a park that includes an Egyptian-style museum of Egyptian antiquities and a planned new museum dedicated to alchemy.

In the 19th century, when academic Egyptology set out to define itself as a serious scholarly pursuit, it rejected outright any idea that ancient Egyptian magic really worked or that Egyptian wisdom could tell us anything today. Most Egyptologists approached their subject matter with dry dispassion, even disdain, as if all those scorpion-charms and snake-oil recipes were just too much to bear. At the same time, alternative interpretations of Egyptian magic found new adherents ready to adapt ancient belief systems to modern times. The Theosophy movement, founded by the Russian writer Helena Blavatsky, was one of several esoteric philosophies that flourished in the late 19th and early 20th centuries. These schools of thought combined elements of South and East Asian religions, chiefly Hinduism and Buddhism, with Hermetic-inspired beliefs in self-realization and secret wisdom that had been revealed to gifted individuals through history. Blavatsky summarized her philosophical thesis in a book called *Isis Unveiled*, whose title gives an indication of the lineage she wished to claim for her ideas. What Isis thinks of the rather long-winded tome has not been recorded.

A contemporary esoteric group that had links to Theosophy, Freemasonry, and Rosicrucianism was called the Hermetic Order of the Golden Dawn. It was organized into temples of Isis-Urania and Amun-Ra and sought to revive magic rites from the distant past, mixing them liberally with astrology, alchemy, and tarot-reading, none of which really had any roots in ancient Egypt. The London chapter of the Golden Dawn, established in 1888, proved to be a social hub whose members at various points included the writers Olivia Shakespear, Edith Nesbit, and Bram Stoker, the poet W. B. Yeats, and Irish revolutionary Maud Gonne. Golden Dawn's most infamous member was Aleister Crowley, a divisive figure during his brief association with the London chapter in the late 1890s. Yeats loathed him, but Crowley soon moved on to new pastures. He travelled to many countries, Egypt among them, developing his own occult following and publishing copious books of his own 'wisdom' – including an Egyptian-inspired tarot guide called *The Book of Thoth*.

Briefly entangled with the Golden Dawn, with its longing for lost wisdom, was a young man named Battiscombe Gunn. Gunn's interest in 'Oriental' languages, including ancient Egyptian, seems to have brought him into the group's orbit, at a time when Crowley was still involved. In 1906, Gunn published a translation of a Middle Kingdom papyrus in the collections of the Bibliothèque Nationale in Paris, on which was written a wisdom text called 'The Instructions of Ptahhotep', a series of maxims passed down by a long-ago sage. These 'instructions' are not magical, but convey the standards of behaviour that were expected of priests and other high-status men in Egypt in language laced with mystical symbols: 'The inner chamber is open for the one who keeps silence' encourages the well-known benefit of guarding your secrets through reference to the importance of secret chambers, and secret knowledge, in Egyptian society.

In the introduction to the translation, which was published in a series called *The Wisdom of the East*, Gunn mused somewhat poetically on what archaeology can – and can't – convey to us about the ancient world:

> Archaeology, is, for those who know her, full of such emotion....Her eyes are sombre with the memory of the wisdom driven from her scattered sanctuaries; and at her lips wonderful things strive for utterance. In her are gathered together the longings and the laughter, the fears and failures, the sins and splendours and achievements of innumerable generations of men; and by her we are shown all the elemental and terrible passions of the unchanging soul of man, to which all cultures and philosophies are but garments to hide its nakedness; and thus in her, as in Art, some of us may realize ourselves.

Years after he left the Golden Dawn, Gunn pursued a career as an academic Egyptologist, studying and working in Berlin, Cairo, Philadelphia, and Oxford. He repudiated his early translation of the Ptahhotep papyrus, embarrassed by its amateur effort but also, presumably, by his admission that 'some of us may realize ourselves' in the quest to understand the 'unchanging soul of man'. Studying ancient wisdom for personal enlightenment was not what a serious scholar was meant to do, and in later life Gunn opposed mystical interpretations of ancient Egyptian thought.

For decades, only a dispassionate approach to magical texts would do, as scholars tried to separate 'magic' from 'medicine', or

Samuel MacGregor Mathers performs an Isis ritual for the
Hermetic Order of the Golden Dawn, which he helped found.

the irrational from the rational. That meant separating Egyptian spells from Greek ones, even where they were written on the same papyrus, or combined in the very same spell; scholars usually specialized in one or the other, and for a long time, Greek was more prestigious as both an ancient language and a scholarly focus. Translations of the written spells also tended to be studied in isolation from material evidence, such as amulets, clay figurines, and birth tusks. Fortunately, in the last twenty-five years, the study of ancient magic has taken a more holistic view. There's certainly no shame in doing what young Battiscombe Gunn did and trying to walk a mile (well, a few cubits) in the sandals of an ancient priest.

Still, modern practitioners who actively worship the Egyptian gods remain apart from Egyptology, even if they draw on academic literature in building their image of the ancient past. Kemetic temples (from *Kemet*, an ancient name for Egypt), found predominantly in the United States, base their worship on some sound research. However, there are many 'alternative' interpretations of ancient Egypt that do the opposite, twisting the evidence for magical practice and other forms of priestly knowledge. Pseudo-scientific theories about astrology, aliens, and the 'true' age of the sphinx and the pyramids have been around for decades (writers Robert Bauval and Graham Hancock have sold millions of books in this vein), and they flourish on the internet. These interpretations inspire sighs of deep frustration in Egyptologists and others who feel passionately about the ancient past, not least because many of the proposals – that only extraterrestrial beings could have built the pyramids, for instance – are rooted in the frankly racist idea that ancient Egyptians were not intelligent enough to have quarried blocks of stone and stacked them up in a solid geometric form.

The inscrutable divine

Today, Egyptian Magic™ comes in a convenient plastic tub – if, that is, you're in the market for an all-purpose skin cream made with olive oil, bee products, and 'divine love', as the ingredients list used to read. Divine love has disappeared from the cream's labels of late. The official bodies that regulate ingredient labelling tend to be sticklers for demonstrable facts, and love of any kind is difficult to measure, much less replicate, in laboratory conditions. However, a dose of divine love fits very well into the ancient aims and marketing claims of the Egyptian Magic™ brand, which brags a formula handed down from 'the great sages, mystics, magicians, and healers' and claims to offer the skin-rejuvenating properties you would expect with such a pedigree. The company's founder, Westley Howard, changed his legal name to LordPharaoh ImHotepAmonRa after a mysterious stranger named Dr Imas revealed the secret formula to him, which is said to be based on an ancient Egyptian recipe. Cue twenty-five years of commercial success, from high street shops to Harrods.

Think what you will of this business's backstory, but there is one thing about it that's as old as the pyramids: Egypt's reputation for magic. In the Book of Exodus, Moses and his brother Aaron confronted the pharaoh's magicians in a battle of miracles, while the astonishing skills of Egypt's priest-magicians were so renowned among the Greeks and Romans, that a white-robed, shaven-headed sorcerer became a fixture in literature and art. Magicians were the heroes of Egyptian tales as well, and Egyptian magic was even credited, after the fact, with the birth of Alexander the Great, whose real father was said to have been an Egyptian pharaoh with magical skills. The ultimate master of magic was the fictional Hermes Trismegistos, admired from Al-Andalus (Islamic Spain) to Renaissance Italy and beyond thanks to his knowledge of ancient wisdom, alchemical promise, and pan-religious appeal.

The kinds of magic and wisdom attributed to these Egyptian wizards didn't involve pulling rabbits out of hats or sawing a shapely assistant in two, although we know that the Old Kingdom magician Djedi could successfully re-attach an animal's head to its body. Most of the superpowers at an ancient magician's command were shaped by far more practical concerns, because a little help from on high went a long way when life went awry. That unseen forces were at work in the world, for good or ill, seemed an obvious conclusion to people when they observed natural phenomena like floods, storms, and shooting stars, or everyday experiences like fevers, dreams, and childbirth. Before there were microscopes, periodic tables, or laws about product labelling, the best way to understand and, if at all possible, influence these unpredictable events was to seek divine intervention via magic – however much it may seem, from a distance, like some kind of superstitious skulduggery.

The imposition of a strict division between science and superstition is a very recent phenomenon. It's an example of the kinds of divisions that occur in a society when things that have been pretty indistinguishable start to rub each other the wrong way. It is in fact very difficult to draw a distinction between 'religion' and 'magic'. Without trying to sort remnants of ancient magical practice into one or the other of these categories, we can start to appreciate it from something that gets us closer to an ancient Egyptian point of view. We've encountered some strange things: disease-causing demons, the cheerful use of crocodile dung, and invisibility spells that probably haven't worked, for those of you who dared to try them (sorry about that). Although there is much, too, that is familiar: labour pains, unrequited passion, or a bad night's sleep.

It would be over-simplifying things to say that the people of ancient Egypt were 'just like us'. Individuals are formed by the society they live in, and every society has its unique ways of being, doing, and thinking. Studying Egyptian magic cannot transport us back in time, turn us into a bird, or make us invisible. But it can give us important insights into the hopes and fears of the people who lived in the time and place we know as ancient Egypt, and add depth to our picture of Egyptian society, whose long lists of kings and rows of similar-looking statues can sometimes seem inscrutable. Inscrutability was part of the point. Scratch the surface, though, and all those sorcerer-princes, proud wizards, and wise women were as vulnerable as any one of us. No doubt they did their level best to help their even more vulnerable clients and colleagues – and faced with fate, who wouldn't wish for a talisman to hold tight to, especially if it came with a dash of Egyptian magic's divine love.

May all your enchantments be enchanting. Very effective. Proven a million times!

FURTHER READING

Organized by chapter, the books, academic articles, and digital resources listed below will point you towards the main sources that I have used to research and write this book. Some of the books and articles are so specialized that you may not be able to access them outside of a major university library; however, I have also tried to include sources that are more readily available. Most research in Egyptology is published in English, German, French, and other European languages. Language is powerful, as any Egyptian magician knew. While I hope readers of this book will have a chance to explore other languages, ancient and modern, I have given preference here to English-language sources, because this book was written for an English-speaking audience.

For ideas presented throughout this book, I owe a particular debt to all of the following, cited in short form in the chapter notes. I recommend these as a starting point for anyone who wants to delve further into the subject.

Jacco Dieleman, *Priests, Tongues, and Rites: The London-Leiden Magical Manuscripts and Translation in Egyptian Ritual (100–300 CE)*, Leiden and Boston: E. J. Brill, 2005.

Marc Etienne, *Heka: Magie et envoûtement dans l'Egypte ancienne*, Paris: Réunion des Musées Nationaux, 2000.

David Frankfurter, *Religion in Roman Egypt: Assimilation and Resistance*, Princeton: Princeton University Press, 1998.

Ludwig D. Morenz, *Hoffen und Handeln: Vom altägyptischen Heka*, Berlin: EB-Verlag Dr. Brandt, 2016.

Geraldine Pinch, *Magic in Ancient Egypt*, London: British Museum Press, 1996, 2nd edn 2006.

Maarten J. Raven, *Egyptian Magic: The Quest for Thoth's Book of Secrets*, Cairo and New York: American University in Cairo Press, 2012.

Robert K. Ritner, *The Mechanics of Ancient Egyptian Magical Practice*, Chicago: Oriental Institute of the University of Chicago, 1993, 2nd edn 2004.

INTRODUCTION

Ramesseum Magician's Tomb: R. B. Parkinson, *The Ramesseum Papyri*, British Museum Online Research Catalogue, 2011, https://www.britishmuseum.org/research/publications/online_research_catalogues/rp/the_ramesseum_papyri.aspx, accessed 5 September 2019; R. B. Parkinson, *Reading Ancient Egyptian Poetry: Among Other Histories*, Malden, MA: Wiley-Blackwell, 2009, pp. 138–72; James E. Quibell, *The Ramesseum*, London: Bernard Quaritch, 1898. **Thinking About Ancient Magic:** Jacco Dieleman, 'Coping with a difficult life: Magic, healing, and sacred knowledge', in Christina Riggs (ed.), *The Oxford Handbook of Roman Egypt*, Oxford: Oxford University Press, 2012, pp. 337–61; David Frankfurter (ed.), *Guide to the Study of Ancient Magic*, Leiden: Brill, 2019. **Conspiracy Against Ramses III:** Ritner, *Mechanics*, pp. 192–214.

CHAPTER 1

Role of Writing in Magic: David Frankfurter, 'The magic of writing and the writing of magic: The power of the word in Egyptian and Greek traditions', *Helios* 21.2 (1994): 189–221. **Pyramid Texts:** James P. Allen with Peter Der Manuelian, *The Ancient Egyptian Pyramid Texts*, Atlanta: Society of Biblical Literature, 2005. **Literacy Rates:** John Baines and C. J. Eyre, 'Four notes on literacy', *Göttinger Miszellen* 61 (1983): 65–96. **The Myth of Isis and Re:** Erik Horning, *Conceptions of God in Ancient Egypt: The One and the Many*, Ithaca, NY: Cornell University Press, 1982, pp. 86–88. Translations include Alexandre Piankoff, *The Litany of Re*, New York: Bollingen Foundation, 1964, pp. 56–59. **Execration Texts and Rituals:** Emmanuel Jambon, 'Les mots et les gestes: Réflexions autour de la place de l'écriture dans un rituel d'envoûtement de l'Égypte pharaonique', *Cahiers "Mondes anciens"* [En ligne] 1 (2010), DOI: 10.4000/mondesanciens.158; Kerry Muhlestein, 'Execration ritual', in Jacco Dieleman and Willeke Wendrich (eds), UCLA Encyclopedia of Egyptology, 2008, http://escholarship.org/uc/item/3f6268zf, accessed 5 September 2019; Ritner, *Mechanics*, pp. 136–80. **Knotting Magic:** Willeke Wendrich, 'Entangled, connected or protected? The power of knots and knotting in Ancient Egypt', in Kasia Szpakowska (ed.), *Through a Glass Darkly: Magic, Dreams and Prophecy in Ancient Egypt*, Swansea: The Classical Press of Wales, 2006, pp. 243–69. **Textual Amulets:** Jacco Dieleman, 'The materiality of textual amulets in ancient Egypt', in Dietrich Boschung and Jan N. Bremmer (eds), *The Materiality of Magic*, Paderborn: Wilhelm Fink, 2015, pp. 23–58; Jacco Dieleman and Hans-W. Fischer-Elfert,

'A textual amulet from Theban Tomb 313 (Papyrus MMA 26.3.225)', *Journal of the American Research Center in Egypt* 53 (2017): 243–57.

CHAPTER 2
Tales of King Khufu and His Sons (Papyrus Westcar): Miriam Lichtheim, *Ancient Egyptian Literature, Vol. I: The Old and Middle Kingdoms*, Los Angeles: University of California Press, 2nd edn 2006, pp. 215–22. **Tales of Setne Khaemwas:** Francis Llewllyn Griffith, *Stories of the High Priests of Memphis*, Oxford: Clarendon Press, 1900; Steve Vinson, *The Craft of a Good Scribe: History, Narrative and Meaning in the First Tale of Setne Khaemwas*, Leiden and Boston: Brill, 2018. **Healing Statues:** László Kákosy, *Egyptian Healing Statues in Three Museums in Italy (Turin, Florence, Naples)*, Turin: Ministero per i beni e le attivita culturali/Museo delle Antichità Egizie, 1999. **The Book Of The Dead:** John H. Taylor, *Journey through the Afterlife: Ancient Egyptian Book of the Dead*, London: British Museum Press, 2010. **Initiation:** Christina Riggs, *Unwrapping Ancient Egypt*, London: Bloomsbury, 2014, pp. 163–85. **Invisibility Spells:** Richard L. Phillips, *In Pursuit of Invisibility: Ritual Texts from Late Roman Egypt*, Durham, NC: American Society of Papyrologists, 2009, p. 117, text 5 (Papyrus Leiden J 395, mid-4th century CE).

CHAPTER 3
The Underworld Books: Erik Hornung, *The Ancient Egyptian Books of the Underworld*, London: Karnak House, 2009. **Demons, Ghosts:** Kasia Szpakowska, 'Demons in the dark: Nightmares and other

nocturnal enemies in ancient Egypt', in Panagiotis Kousoulis (ed.), *Ancient Egyptian Demonology: Studies on the Boundaries between the Demonic and the Divine in Ancient Egyptian Magic*, Leuven: Peeters, 2011, pp. 63–76; Kasia Szpakowska, 'Demons in ancient Egypt', *Religion Compass* 3 (2009): 799–805, DOI:10.1111/j.1749-8171.2009.00169.x. **Visits to Tomb Chapels:** Melinda Hartwig (ed.), *The Tomb Chapel of Menna (Theban Tomb 69): The Art, Culture, and Science of Painting in an Egyptian Tomb*, Cairo and New York: American University of Cairo Press, 2013, pp. 165–74. **Ancestor Worship:** Nicola Harrington, *Living with the Dead: Ancestor Worship and Mortuary Ritual in Ancient Egypt*, Oxford: Oxbow, 2013. **Spell Against Nightmares; Clay Cobras:** Robert K. Ritner, 'O. Gardiner 363: A spell against night terrors', *Journal of the American Research Centre in Egypt* 27 (1990): 25–41; Kasia Szpakowska, 'Playing with fire: Initial observations on the religious uses of clay cobras from Amarna', *Journal of the American Research Center in Egypt* 40 (2003): 113–22. **Letters to the Dead:** Richard Parkinson, *Voices from Ancient Egypt: An Anthology of Middle Kingdom Writings*, London: British Museum Press, 1991, p. 142, no. 55 (letter from Merertifi to Nebitef); Edward Wente, *Letters from Ancient Egypt*, Atlanta: Scholars Press, 1990, p. 215, no. 349 (letter from Merertifi to Nebitef); p. 213, no. 344 (from son to his parents); pp. 216–17, no. 352 (long diatribe to deceased wife). **Mummy Fiction:** Bradley Deane, 'Mummy fiction and the occupation of Egypt: Imperial striptease', *English Literature in Translation, 1880–1920* 51. 4 (2008):

381–410; Roger Luckhurst, *The Mummy's Curse: The True History of a Dark Fantasy*, Oxford: Oxford University Press, 2012. **Methods and Meaning of Mummification:** Salima Ikram, 'Mummification', in Willeke Wendrich (ed.), *UCLA Encyclopedia of Egyptology*, 2010, http://escholarship. org/uc/item/0gn7x3ff, accessed 5 September 2019; Maarten J. Raven, 'Egyptian concepts on the orientation of the human body', *Journal of Egyptian Archaeology* 91 (2005): 37–53; Christina Riggs, *Unwrapping Ancient Egypt*, London: Bloomsbury, pp. 77–108. **Khoiak Festival and 'Corn Mummies':** Maria Centrone, 'Corn-Mummies, amulets of life', in Kasia Szpakowska (ed.), *Through a Glass Darkly: Magic, Dreams and Prophecy in Ancient Egypt*, Swansea: The Classical Press of Wales, 2006, pp. 33–45; Maarten J. Raven, 'A new type of Osiris burials', in Willy Clarysse, Antoon Schoors and Harco Willems (eds), *Egyptian Religion: The Last Thousand Years. Studies Dedicated to the Memory of Jan Quaegebeur*, Leuven: Peeters, 1998, pp. 227–39.

CHAPTER 4

Representation of Egyptian Deities: Erik Horning, *Conceptions of God in Ancient Egypt: The One and the Many*, Ithaca, NY: Cornell University Press, 1982; Richard H. Wilkinson, *The Complete Gods and Goddesses of Ancient Egypt*, London and New York: Thames & Hudson, 2003. **Animals in Egyptian Art:** Dorothea Arnold, *An Egyptian Bestiary*, New York: Metropolitan Museum of Art, 1995; Philippe Germond and Jacques Livet, *An Egyptian Bestiary: Animals in Life and Religion in the Land of the*

Pharaohs, London: Thames & Hudson, 2001. **Demons with Foreign-Sounding Names:** Susanne Beck, *Exorcism, Illness and Demons in an Ancient Egyptian Context: The Egyptian Magical Papyrus Leiden I 343 + 345*, Leiden: Sidestone Press, 2018. **Demon (Epagomenal) Days:** Maarten J. Raven, 'Charms for protection during the epagomenal days', in Jacobus van Dijk (ed.), *Essays on Ancient Egypt in Honour of Herman Te Velde*, Groningen: Styx, 1997, pp. 275–91. **Seth Animal:** Angela McDonald, 'Tall tails: The Seth animal reconsidered', in Angela McDonald and Christins Riggs (eds), *Current Research in Egyptology*, Oxford: Archaeopress, 2000, pp. 75–81. **The God Tutu:** Olaf E. Kaper, *The Egyptian God Tutu: A Study of the Sphinx-God and Master of Demons*, Leuven: Peeters, 2003. **Water Spells:** Ritner, *Mechanics*, pp. 226–31. **Animal Mummies:** Edward Bleiberg and Yekaterina Barbash, *Soulful Creatures: Animal Mummies in Ancient Egypt*, London: Giles, 2013; Salima Ikram (ed.), *Divine Creatures: Animal Mummies in Ancient Egypt*, Cairo and New York: American University in Cairo Press, 2005. **Ipet (Great Bear):** Horst Beinlich, *Der Mythos in seiner Landscaft: Das ägyptisches 'Buch vom Fayum'*, Dettelbach: J. H. Röll, 2013. **Dwarfs:** Veronique Dasen, *Dwarfs in Ancient Egypt and Greece*, Oxford: Clarendon Press, 1993, 2nd edn 2013; S. van Erp, 'Pataikos: A Forgotten Amulet', MA thesis, Universiteit Leiden, 2014, with further literature.

CHAPTER 5
Medicine in Ancient Egypt:
James P. Allen, *The Art of Medicine in Ancient Egypt*, New York: Metropolitan Museum of Art, 2005; Paul Ghalioungui, *The Physicians of Pharaonic Egypt*, Cairo: Al-Ahram Center for Scientific Translations, 1983; John F. Nunn, *Ancient Egyptian Medicina*, London: British Museum Press, 1996. **Metternich Stela:** Photographs, translation and further references on the museum website, https://www.metmuseum.org/art/ collection/search/546037, accessed 5 September 2019. **Scale and Magical Objects:** Jane Draycott, 'Size matters: Reconsidering Horus on the crocodiles in miniature', *Pallas* [En ligne] 86 (2011), DOI: 10.4000/pallas.2124; Ian S. Moyer and Jacco Dieleman, 'Miniaturization and the Opening of the Mouth in a Greek magical text (PGM XII.270–350)', *Journal of Ancient Near Eastern Religions* 3.1 (2003): 47–72. **Knotting Spell for Headache:** Willeke Wendrich, 'Entangled, connected or protected?', in Kasia Szpakowska (ed.), *Through a Glass Darkly: Magic, Dreams and Prophecy in Ancient Egypt*, Swansea: The Classical Press of Wales, 2006, pp. 250–51 (Leiden Magical Papyrus I 348). **Spell for Taking Medicine:** J. F. Borghouts, *Ancient Egyptian Magical Texts*, Leiden: Brill, 1978 p. 45, text 72 (adapted). **Contendings of Horus and Seth:** Ellen F. Morris, 'Sacred and obscene laughter in the "Contendings of Horus and Seth", in Egyptian inversions of everyday life, and in the context of cultic competition', in Thomas Schneider and Kasia Szpakowska (eds), *Egyptian Stories: A British Egyptological Tribute to Alan B. Lloyd*, Münster: Ugarit, pp. 197–224. **Bilingual Papyri, List of Ingredients:** Dieleman, *Priests, Tongues, and Rites*, pp. 189–94. **Coffins of Padiamenipet and Kleopatra:** Christina Riggs, 'Archaism

and artistic sources in Roman Egypt: The coffins of the Soter family and the temple of Deir el-Medina', *Bulletin de l'Institut français d'archéologie orientale* 106 (2006): 315–32. **Imhotep and Amenhotep, Son of Hapu:** Dietrich Wildung, *Egyptian Saints: Deification in Pharaonic Egypt*, New York: New York University Press, 1977.

CHAPTER 6

Sex, Sexuality, Love Poetry: Renata Landgráfová and Hana Navrátilová, *Sex and the Golden Goddess, Vol. I: Ancient Egyptian love songs in context*, Prague: Czech Institute of Egyptology, 2009 (songs quoted are at pp. 155, 163, and 168–69); Renata Landgráfová and Hana Navrátilová (eds), *Sex and the Golden Goddess, Vol. II: World of the Love Songs*, Prague: Czech Institute of Egyptology, 2015; Lise Manniche, *Sexual Life in Ancient Egypt*, London: Kegan Paul, 2nd edn 2002. **Spell to Attract a Woman:** J. F. Borghouts, *Ancient Egyptian Magical Texts*, Leiden: Brill, 1978, p. 1, text 1. **Wax Crocodile (Papyrus Westcar, Khufu Tales):** Lise Manniche, *An Ancient Egyptian Herbal*, London: British Museum Press, 1989, pp. 60–62; Pinch, *Magic*, pp. 96–97. **Impotence Cure:** Lise Manniche, *Sexual Life in Ancient Egypt*, London: Kegan Paul, 2nd edn 2002, p. 103. **Aphrodisiac with Shrewmouse:** Dieleman, *Priests, Tongues, and Rites*, p. 95 (adapted). **Childless Couple:** Gay Robins, *Women in Ancient Egypt*, London: British Museum Press, 1993, p. 77. **Contraceptives:** Lise Manniche, *An Ancient Egyptian Herbal*, London: British Museum Press, 1989. **Spell Against Vaginal Bleeding:** J. F. Borghouts, *Ancient Egyptian Magical Texts*, Leiden: Brill, 1978, p. 24, text 31

(adapted). **Spells for Childbirth:** J. F. Borghouts, *Ancient Egyptian Magical Texts*, Leiden: Brill, 1978, p. 39, nos 60, 61 (adapted). **Birth Bricks:** Ann Macy Roth and Catharine H. Roehrig, 'Magical bricks and the bricks of birth', *Journal of Egyptian Archaeology* 88 (2002): 121–39; Josef Wegner, 'A decorated birth-brick from South Abydos: New evidence on childbirth and birth magic in the Middle Kingdom', in David P. Silverman et al. (eds), *Archaism and Innovation: Studies in the Culture of Middle Kingdom Egypt*, New Haven: Yale University Press, 2009, pp. 447–96. **Birth Arbors, Vines:** Lise Manniche, *An Ancient Egyptian Herbal*, London: British Museum Press, 1989, pp. 84–85, 99, 168–70; Lynn Meskell, *Private Life in New Kingdom Egypt*, Princeton: Princeton University Press, 2002, pp. 110–21. **Amarna Royal Tomb:** Geoffrey T. Martin, *The Royal Tomb at El-Amarna, Vol. II: The Reliefs, Inscriptions, and Architecture*, London: Egypt Exploration Society, 1989, pp. 46–48. **Birth Tusks:** Stephen Quirke, *Birth Tusks: The Armoury of Health in Context, Egypt 1800 BC*, London: Golden House Publications, 2016. **Knot-Spell for Baby:** J. F. Borghouts, *Ancient Egyptian Magical Texts*, Leiden: Brill, 1978, pp. 42–43, text 68 (adapted). **Opening the Mouth and Childbirth:** Ann Macy Roth, 'The *pšs-kf* and the "Opening of the Mouth" ceremony: a ritual of birth and rebirth', *Journal of Egyptian Archaeology* 78 (1992): 113–47; Ann Macy Roth, 'Fingers, stars, and the "Opening of the Mouth": the nature and function of the *ntrwj*-blades', *Journal of Egyptian Archaeology* 79 (1993): 57–79. **Birth Temples:** Holgar Kockelmann, 'Mammisi (Birth House)', in Willeke Wendrich (ed.),

UCLA Encyclopedia of Egyptology, 2011, https://escholarship.org/uc/item/8xj4k0ww, accessed 5 September 2019. **Female Figurines:** Elizabeth A. Waraksa, 'Female figurines (Pharaonic Period),' in Willeke Wendrich (ed.), *UCLA Encyclopedia of Egyptology*, 2008, http://escholarship.org/uc/item/4dg0d57b, accessed 5 September 2019; Elizabeth A. Waraksa, *Female Figurines from the Mut Precinct: Context and Ritual Function*, Fribourg: Vandenhoeck & Ruprecht, 2009.

CHAPTER 7
Dream Interpretation: Kasia Szpakowska, 'Dream interpretation in the Ramesside age', in Mark Collier and Steven Snape (eds), *Ramesside Studies in Honour of K. A. Kitchen*, Bolton: Rutherford Press, 2011, pp. 509–17. **Demotic Dream Spell of Osiris:** Jacco Dieleman, 'Scribal practices in the production of magic handbooks in Egypt', in Shaul Shaked et al. (eds), *Continuity and Innovation in the Magical Tradition*, Leiden: Brill, 2011, pp. 85–117 (at p. 109). **Calendars of Unlucky Days:** Gerald E. Kadish, 'Calendar of lucky and unlucky days', in Roger S. Bagnall et al. (eds), *The Encyclopedia of Ancient History*, Malden, MA: Wiley-Blackwell, 2013, pp. 1265–66, DOI: 10.1002/9781444338386.wbeah2107; examples taken from Raven, *Egyptian Magic*, p. 106. **Spell Against Demon (Epagomenal) Days:** Adapted from Raven, *Egyptian Magic*, p. 105. **New Year Flasks:** Aurélia Masson, 'New Year's flasks', in Alexandra Villing et al., *Naukratis: Greeks and Egyptians*, The British Museum online, no date, https://www.britishmuseum.org/research/online_research_catalogues/

ng/naukratis_greeks_in_egypt/material_culture_of_naukratis/new_years_flasks.aspx, accessed 5 September 2019. **Oracles:** Andreas Effland, '"You will open up the ways in the underworld of the god": Aspects of Roman and Late Antique Abydos', in Elizabeth O'Connell (ed.), *Egypt in the First Millennium AD: Perspectives from New Fieldwork*, Leuven: Peeters, 2014, pp. 193–205; Frankfurter, *Religion in Roman Egypt,* pp. 145–97; Ritner, *Mechanics*, pp. 214–18; Gaëlle Tallet, 'Oracles', in Christina Riggs (ed.), *The Oxford Handbook of Roman Egypt*, Oxford: Oxford University Press, 2012, pp. 398–415. **Divination:** Jacco Dieleman, 'Scribal practices in the production of magic handbooks in Egypt', in Shaul Shaked et al. (eds), *Continuity and Innovation in the Magical Tradition*, Leiden: Brill, 2011, p. 99; Joachim Friedrich Quack, 'A black cat from the right, and a scarab on your head: New sources for ancient Egyptian dream divination', in Kasia Szpakowska (ed.), *Through a Glass Darkly: Magic, Dreams and Prophecy in Ancient Egypt*, Swansea: The Classical Press of Wales, 2006, pp. 175–87. **Statue of Harkhebi:** Jacco Dieleman, 'Claiming the stars: Egyptian priests facing the sky', in Susanne Bickel and Antonio Loprieno (eds), *Aegyptiaca Helvetica 17: Basel Egyptology Prize*, Basel: Schwabe, 2003, pp. 277–89. **Dendera Zodiac:** Overview on museum website, https://www.louvre.fr/en/oeuvre-notices/zodiac-dendera, accessed 5 September 2019; Sylvie Cauville, *Le Zodiaque d'Osiris*, Leuven: Peeters, 1997; Diane Greco Josefowicz and Jed Buchwald, *The Zodiac of Paris: How an Improbable Controversy Over an Ancient Egyptian Artifact Provoked* a *Modern Debate Between Religion and Science*, Princeton: Princeton University Press, 2010.

CHAPTER 8
Ancient Egypt in Roman Italy:
Caitlín Eilís Barrett, 'Egypt in Roman visual and material culture', *Oxford Handbooks Online*, DOI: 10.1093/oxfordhb/9780199935390.013.18; Molly Swetnam-Burland, *Egypt in Italy: Visions of Egypt in Roman Imperial Culture*, Cambridge and New York: Cambridge University Press, 2015.
Greek and Roman Views of Egypt:
Stephen Nimis, 'Egypt in Greco-Roman history and fiction', *Alif: Journal of Comparative Poetics* 24 (2004): 34–67; Ian Rutherford, 'Kalasiris and Setne Khamwas: A Greek novel and some Egyptian models', *Zeitschrift für Papyrologie un Epigraphik* 117 (1997): 203–9. **Philae Temple:** Jitse H. F. Dijkstra, 'Horus on his throne: The holy falcon of Philae in his demonic cage', *Göttinger Miszellen* 189 (2002): 7–10; Jitse H. F. Dijkstra, *Philae and the End of Ancient Egyptian Religion: A Regional Study of Religious Transformation (298–642 CE)*, Leuven: Peeters, 2008.
Magic Gems: Ian S. Moyer and Jacco Dieleman, 'Miniaturization and the Opening of the Mouth in a Greek magical text (PGM XII.270–350)', *Journal of Ancient Near Eastern Religions* 3.1 (2003): 47–72. **Alchemy; Hermes Trismegistos:** Garth Fowden, *The Egyptian Hermes: A Historical Approach to the Late Pagan Mind*, Princeton: Princeton University Press, 2nd edn, 1993; Kevin van Bladel, *The Arabic Hermes: From Pagan Sage to Prophet of Science*, Oxford and New York: Oxford University Press, 2009.
Rosicrucians, Freemasons: Erik

Hornung, *The Secret Lore of Egypt: Its Impact on the West*, Ithaca, NY: Cornell University Press, 2001; Christina Riggs, *Egypt: Lost Civilizations*, London: Reaktion, 2017; Frances Yates, *The Rosicrucian Enlightenment*, London and New York: Routledge, 2000 [1972].
Hermetic Order of The Golden Dawn: David Gange, *Dialogues with the Dead: Egyptology in British Culture and Religion 1822–1922*, Oxford: Oxford University Press, 2013, pp. 262–69; Steven Vinson and Janet Gunn, 'Studies in esoteric syntax: the enigmatic friendship of Aleister Crowley and Battiscombe Gunn', in William Carruthers (ed.), *Histories of Egyptology: Interdisciplinary Measures*, London and New York: Routledge, 2015, pp. 96–112. **Gunn, Instructions of Ptahhotep:** 'Introduction', http://www.gutenberg.org/files/30508/30508-h/30508-h.htm, accessed 5 September 2019. **Kemetic Religion:** Paul Harrison, *Profane Egyptologists: The Modern Revival of Ancient Egyptian Religion*, London: UCL Institute of Archaeology/Routledge, 2017. **Egyptian Magic™:** https://egyptianmagic.com, accessed 5 September 2019.

SOURCES OF ILLUSTRATIONS

8 James Edward Quibell, *The Ramesseum*, plate III (London, B. Quaritch, 1898); 15 Universal History Archive/Getty; 16 The Metropolitan Museum of Art, New York. Gift of J. Pierpont Morgan, 1911; 22 World History Archive/Alamy; 26 Brooklyn Museum, New York; 30 Egyptian Museum, Cairo; 32 The Metropolitan Museum of Art, New York. Rogers Fund, 1926; 35 Egyptian National Museum, Cairo, Egypt/ Bridgeman Images; 36 Bridgeman Images; 40 The Metropolitan Museum of Art, New York. Anonymous Gift, 1926; 45 The British Museum, London; 46–47 The Trustees of the British Museum; 52 World History Archive/Alamy; 54 Photo RMN-Grand Palais (Musée du Louvre/Les frères Chuzeville); 59 Photo Musée du Louvre, Dist. RMN-Grand Palais/Georges Poncet; 62–63 The British Museum, London; 69 Asaf Braverman; 76 Bridgeman Images; 78 The Metropolitan Museum of Art Purchase, Fletcher Fund and The Guide Foundation Inc. Gift, 1966; 80, 81 The Metropolitan Museum of Art, New York. Rogers Fund, 1936; 82 The Metropolitan Museum of Art, New York. Rogers Fund, 1927; 84 The Metropolitan Museum of Art, New York. Gift of Edward S. Harkness, 1917; 89 The Metropolitan Museum of Art, New York. Purchase, Edward S. Harkness Gift, 1926; 91 The Trustees of the British Museum; 93 Heritage Image Partnership Ltd/Alamy; 94 The Trustees of the British Museum; 97 The Griffith Institute, Oxford; 98 The Metropolitan Museum of Art, New York. Rogers Fund, 1930; 100 The Metropolitan Museum of Art, New York. Harris Brisbane Dick Fund, 1956; 102 The Metropolitan Museum of Art, New York. Purchase, Edward S. Harkness Gift, 1926; 103 Brooklyn Museum of Art, New York; 104 The Walters Art Museum, Baltimore. Acquired by Henry Walters, before 1931; 107 Museo Egizio, Turin; 108, 109 The Walters Art Museum, Baltimore. Museum purchase, 1949, and Gift of the Morgan Library & Museum; 111 The Metropolitan Museum of Art, New York. Gift of Egypt Exploration Fund; 113 The Metropolitan Museum of Art, New York. Edith Perry Chapman Fund, 1958; 114 Valley of the Queens, Thebes, Egypt; 115 The Trustees of the British Museum; 118, 120 The Metropolitan Museum of Art, New York. Fletcher Fund, 1950; 121 Egyptian Museum, Cairo; 125 The J. Paul Getty Museum, Los Angeles; 133 The Trustees of the British Museum; 134 The Metropolitan Museum of Art, New York. Purchase, Edward S. Harkness Gift, 1926; 137 Werner Forman/ Universal Images Group/Getty Images; 138–39 The Metropolitan Museum of Art, New York. Rogers Fund, 1930; 143 Dunhill/Shutterstock; 144 The Metropolitan Museum of Art, New York. Rogers Fund, 1931; 147 Musée du Louvre, Paris; 152 James Edward Quibell, Tomb of Yuaa and Thuiu, plate XLI (Le Caire: Impr. de l'Institut français d'archéologie orientale, 1908); 154 Courtesy of the Penn Museum, Philadelphia; 156–57 The Metropolitan Museum of Art, New York. Theodore M. Davis Collection, Bequest of Theodore M. Davis, 1915; 159 The Metropolitan Museum of Art, New York. Rogers Fund, 1944; 160 The Metropolitan Museum of Art, New York. Gift of Edward S. Harkness, 1928; 165 Brooklyn Museum, New York; 169 The Metropolitan Museum of Art, New York. Theodore M. Davis Collection, Bequest of Theodore M. Davis, 1915; 171 The Metropolitan Museum of Art, New York. Rogers Fund, 1921; 176 The Metropolitan Museum of Art, New York. Rogers Fund, 1948; 179 Rare Book Division, New York Public Library; 183 akg-images; 185 The Metropolitan Museum of Art, New York. Gift of Miss Helen Miller Gould, 1910; 187 Science History Images/Alamy

INDEX

Page numbers in *italics*
refer to illustrations

Aaron *40*, 41–42, 193
Abraxas 185, 186
afterlife 66–70, 74, 83, 175
Aha 157
Aker 102
Akhenaten, King 156
Akhet 90–91, 167
akhu 17, 71, 72, 74, 112
alchemy 188, 189
Alexander the Great 181,
    193
Ali, Mohammed 119
aloe 129
Amenhotep, son of Hapu
    131–35, *133*, *169*
Amenhotep III 101, 132
Ammut 65, 109
amulet-makers 55–56, 124
amulets 55–56, 90, 184;
    baby's first 157–58; cats
    99; demon days 91, *91*,
    167, 168; faience 124–25;
    funerary 79–81, *80*,
    81, 83; healing 124–25,
    125, 126; hieroglyphs as
    33–34, 37; Horus, Isis and
    Nephthys *89*; Horus-
    on-the-crocodiles 124;
    mummification rites *78*,
    79–81; papyrus 32–33, *32*,
    56; regeneration and 70;
    scarab beetles 110; *tyet*-
    amulets 56
Amun 87, 88, 112, 132
Amun-Ra 103, 172, 189
ancestral spirits 70–71
animals: mummification
    100, 101, 106, 112;
    protective 95–110; real
    and fantastic 92, *93*; *see
    also* individual species

ankh 33–34, *35*
Ankhiry 74
Anubis 21, *76*, 96, 149
Apep 68, 99, 105, 164
Asiatics 27
Astarte 90
astrology 189
astronomy 175–80
Atum 168

ba 112
baboons 7, 112, 130, 157
balsams 78–79
Bastet 57–60, *59*, 99, 119
bau 103
Baufre, Prince 43
Bes *152*; as a protector 88,
    90, 155, *165*, 166; birth
    temples 161; childbirth
    151, 155, 161; Metternich
    Stela 119, *120*, 121; oracle
    at Abydos 174–75, 181;
    stela with Tutu and *103*
birds 92, 111–13; *see also*
    individual species
birth bricks 153–55, *154*,
    157
birth-houses *160*, 161
birth tusks 156–57, *156–57*
birthwort 155–56
Blavatsky, Helena 188–89
Book of the Dead 61,
    62–63, 64, 70, 99, 154
Book of the Fayum *108*,
    109
Book of Thoth 46, 47,
    48–50, 60, 127
The Book of Thoth (tarot
    guide) 189
bound prisoner
    figures 26–28, *26*, 29
British Museum, London
    131
burials 66, 70–71

calendar of good and bad
    days 167, 170
Cambyses 101
Carter, Howard 79
cartouches 34, *36*
cats *98*, 99–101, 106, 112,
    130, 157, 164
cemeteries 70–71
childbirth 57, 95, 109,
    110, 136, 138–40, 150–57,
    159–61, 163
children: caring for 95,
    136; mortality and
    healing 122–23;
    mummies 125, *125*;
    protective deities 90, 109
cobras 7, 72, 105, 121
Coffin Texts 61, 70, 145
coffins 75; coffin
    paintings of Kleopatra
    132, *133*, 135; decoration
    81, 177; *wedjat*-eyes 122
Constantius II 175
constellations 79, 175–77,
    178
The Contendings of Horus
    and Seth 127
contraception 148–49, 158
coriander 129
crocodiles 10, *32*, 33, 106,
    109, 112, 115, 130, 131, 141,
    145, 185, *185*
Crowley, Aleister 189
curses 24–29

Dakhla Oasis 103
dead: dealing with the
    dead 66–83; infant and
    child mortality 150
decans 79, 175, 178
Deir el-Medina 71, *76*, *94*,
    98, 106, 135, 148, 155, 163
demon days 91, *91*, 167–68
demons 90

Dendera zodiac *179*, 181, 189–90
Denon, Vivant 180
deposits, ritual 28–29
Diodorus of Sicily 77, 101
diseases 12, 116–35
divination manuals 173
Djadjaemankh 43, 50, 53
djed medu 13–39
djed pillar 21, 22, 80; amulets 80, 96
Djedi 43–44, 50, 194
Djehutyhotep *54*, 55
Djoser, King 132
dogs 99
dreams 163–66, 170, 174
Duat 67–70, 74, 83, 175

Egyptian Magic™ 193
Egyptian Museum, Turin 142
embalming 75, 77–80, *78*, *121*
epagomenal days 91, *91*
execration rituals 26–29, 38–39
Exodus 41, 43, 193
Eye of Horus (*wedjat*) 121, 178

faience 56, 80; amulets 124; bowls 142; feeding cups 158, *159*; hippopotami *84*, 85–86, 87, 95
falcons 112–13, 184
Fayum Oasis 106
feathers 111, 112, 113, 115
feeding cups 158, *159*
fertility 136, 142, 148
festivals 170
figures: clay figure of naked women 146–48, *147*; execration 26–27, *26*, 28, 38–39; hippopotami *84*, 85–86, 87, 95; wax 12, 14, 48
flasks, New Year's 168, *169*, 170

flax plant 129
Four Sons of Horus 80–81, *82*, *121*
Freemasonry 188, 189
funeral rites 66, 67
future, predicting the 162–80

gems, magical 185–86, *185*
genies 90
gods and goddesses 20–21, 50, 182; animal forms 86, 87; characteristics 88; childbirth 136; minor 88; name references 24; *netjer* 87–88; *see also* individual gods and goddesses
Golden Dawn 189–90
Great Bear constellation *108*, 109–10, 175
Great Pyramid, Giza 43, 102
greywacke 58
Gunn, Battiscombe 189–90, 192
Gurob 71

Hapu 132, *133*
Hardedef, Prince 43
Harkhebi 177–78
Hathor 24, 87; animal forms 88; centre of worship 88; childbirth 150–51, 155, *160*; Eye of Horus 121; hieroglyphic symbols 88; offerings to 142; return to Egypt 141, 142; Seven Hathors 163; *shesheshat* 144; temple of 135, *137*, 178, *179*
headaches 32
headrests *165*, 166
healing 32, 116–35
heka (magic) 6, 12, 23, 24, 43, 53, *54*, 55, 56–57, 126, 127, 172

Heka (god) 172
Heliodoros 184
herbal medicines 127–29
Herculaneum 182, *183*
Hermes the Three-Times-Great (Hermes Trismegistos) 186, *187*, 193
Hermetic Order of the Golden Dawn 189, *191*
Herodotus 37, 130, 173
hery-seshta ('master of secrets') 96
hieratic script 9, 18
hieroglyphics: as amulets and emblems 33–37; *djed medu* 14, *16*, 17–19; symbolic power of 37–38
hippopotami 92, 106, 109, 130; faience *84*, 85–86, 87, 95; goddesses *108*, 151, 178; birth tusk 156–57, *156–57*; ivories 7, 95
Horapollo 37–38
horoscopes 177–78
Horus 17, 87, 182; amulet of *89*; avenges father 122; childbirth 150, 151, 153; childhood as healing inspiration 117; The Contendings of Horus and Seth 127; demon days 91; falcon form 88, 113; Four Sons of Horus 80–81, *82*, *121*; human and animal forms 86, 88, 113; invitations to visit via dreams 165; and Isis 21, 24, 60, 122, 138, 161; Metternich Stela *118*, 119–23, *120*, 124, 151, 168; myths 21, 23, 24, 60; Opening of the Mouth ritual 159; the planets 177; scorpions and 111; spells 24, 126; temple of 113, 184

Horus-on-the-crocodiles:
  healing stela 58, *59*, 60;
  Metternich Stela *118*,
  119–23, *120*, 124, 151, 168
hour-priests 175, 177–78
House of Life 57–61, 64
households, protection
  of 90
Howard, Westley 193

ibex 130
ibis 112, *113*, 123
Ibn Wahshiyya 38
Ikhweret 47, 48, 49, 50
illiteracy 18
illness 53, 55, 72, 116–35
Imhotep 117, 131–35, *133*,
  134, 182
impotence 145
incense 77
incubation 166
initiation rites 61, *64*
Ipet 109
Isis 17, 37, 87; amulet
  of *89*; coffin for 156;
  childbirth 150, 151;
  constellations associated
  with 175; demon days
  91; Hermetic Order of
  the Golden Dawn *191*;
  hieroglyphic symbols
  88; and Horus 21, 24,
  60, 122, 138, 161; human
  and animal forms 86,
  88; invitations to visit
  via dreams 165; magic
  23; Metternich Stela 121,
  122–23; myths 34, 38, 60;
  Opening of the Mouth
  ritual 159; as protector
  10; red kite form 113,
  114; secrecy and myths
  20–23; snakes and 105;
  solar eclipse 178; spells
  24; temples dedicated to
  182, *183*, 184; *tyet* knot 33
Isis-Urania, temple of 189
Iufaa *169*

jackals 6, 92, 96, *97*, 115
Jehovah 41
judgment ceremonies 61,
  62–63, 64
Juvenal 87

Kemetic temples 192
Khaemwaset, Prince 44–
  46, *45*, 50
Khafre, Prince 145
Khufu, King 43–44, 46,
  145, 154
kings, Egyptian 42–44;
  see also individual kings
Kleopatra 131–32, *133*, 135
knots 31–34, 39, 56, 115,
  126, 149
Kush 27

laxatives 128, 129
letters to the dead 73–74
linen 31–32, 56, 91, 129,
  149
lions 7, 92, 102, 109, 115,
  130, 155, 157
literacy 18–19, 61
lotus flowers 9, 142, *143*
Louvre, Paris 131, *179*, 180
love 141–47
lovesickness 136, 140, 145
lunar eclipse 178
lust 145, 146

maat 29, 162, 164
Maat (goddess) 113
magician's tomb 6–11, *8*,
  96, 155, 156
Mahes 58, 60
malevolent spirits 72–73
manuals: dream 165–66,
  170, 173; magic 173, 185
medicine men 131–35
medicines 126–31
mediums 173
Meketaten, Princess 156
memorial shrines 71–72
Menna, tomb of *138–39*
Meretseger 105–6, *107*

Meskhenet 153–54
Metropolitan Museum
  of Art, New York 86
Metternich Stela *118*,
  119–23, *120*, 151
Metternich-Winneberg,
  Prince von 119
midwives 136, 153, 159
Mirgissa 28
mirrors 34, *35*
miscarriage 31–32,
  149–50, 173
Mnevis bull 119
Montu 172
Moses *40*, 41–42, 186, 193
motherhood 109, 110
mummies *185*; magical
  74–83; Padiamenipet
  and Kleopatra 131–32
mummification 67,
  77–80, *121*, 175; amulets
  78, 79–81; animals *100*,
  101, 106, 112; goal of
  74, 75; natron 7, 77–78;
  origin-story for 21; the
  poor and 66, 83; use of
  linen 31
Mut 23, 60, 112
mwtw 72–73, 74, 90
myths 19–20

names, Egyptian 23–24
Naneferkaptah 46–47,
  48–50, 60
natron 7, 77–78
Nectanebo II, King 119
Nefertiti, Queen 156
Nefertum 121
Neith 109
Nekhbet *104*, 105, *107*,
  112, 121
nemes headdress 102
Nephthys *89*, 91, 113, *114*,
  165
Nesbit, Edith 189
Nesu-Atum 119
netjer (god) 88
netjery tool 159

New Year's flask 168, *169*, 170

newborn babies 157–61

Newton, Isaac 188

night sky, tomb and coffin decorations 175–77, *176*

nightmares 165

Nile Delta 26, 71

Nile valley 25, 96

Nilometers 162

Nubia 27

Nut 110, 113

obsidian 77

ointments 128

'Opening of the Mouth' ritual 53, 159

oracles 170–75, *171*

oral traditions 19

Osiris 61, 68, 86, 87; Abydos 88, 174; Anubis and 96; calling the dead by name of 24; centre of worship 88, 174; crocodiles 106; demon days 91; hippos 95; invitations to visit via dreams 165–66; murder of 113, 122; myths 21, 23; scarab beetles 110

Padiamenipet 131–32, 135

Padimahes 58, *59*, 60–61

palettes 92

papyrus 18; amulets 32–33, *32*, 56, 91, *91*; demon days spell 167–68; healing ingredients 130–31; knotted 126; Setne story *46–47*; spells to treat injuries or illness 116–17; Turin papyrus 142; winged god with protective flames 115, *115*

Pasheribastet 58, *59*, 60–61

Pasherimut 58, *59*, 60–61

peh-netjer (oracle) 165, 170, 172

pekher (remedy) 119

Peret 90

peshes-kef tool 159

pessaries 128, 148

Philae, temple of 37

pigs 115

placebo effect 116, 126

planets 177

Pliny the Elder 129

Polyaenus 101

portable magic 123–26

poultices 128

pregnancy 136, 138, 139, 148–50

priests 50–51, 53–65, 184; astronomy 175; cemetery 71; hour-priests 175, 177–78; House of Life 57–61, 64; *kherep* of Serket 55, 56; *khery-heb* 53, 79; reading-priests 140, 184; scorpion-charmers 55, 56, 110, 124, 177, 184; *sem*-priests 44, 50, *52*, 53, 159; *wab*-priests 53

prisoner figures 26–28, *26*, 29

protective magic 32, 33–37, 39

Ptah 44

Pyramid Texts 14–17, 23, 24, 25, 38, 42, 61, 87–88

pyramids 14, 43, 102, 192

Qenherkhepeshef 163, 173

quadrupeds 95

Qudshu 90

Ra 87, 102, 110, 182; Bastet and 99; Book of Thoth 48, 49; centre of worship 88; cult of 127; demon days 167–68; Duat 68, *69*, 90; human and animal forms 86, 88, 113; Isis and 20, 23, 105;

Metternich Stela 123; Mnevis bull 119; myths 34, 38; regeneration of 142

Ra-Horakhty 121

Ramesseum tomb 7–11, *8*, 96, 155, 156

rams 102, 115

Ramses II, King 7, 44, 163

Ramses III, King 12

Ramses IX, King 172

reading-priests 140, 184

red kite 112–13, *114*

red lettering 18, 19

Redjedet 44, 153

rekh-khet (magician) 55, 57

rekhet (magician) 57

remedies, magical 126–31

Renenutet 105

reproduction 145

reptiles 92, 105–10

rituals: curse rituals 38–39; ritual events 28–29; three components of 13

romance 141–44

Rosicrucianism 188, 189

Sa-Osiris 66–67, 71, 83

Samanu 90

Saqqara 46, 47, 49, 50, 132

sau (amulet-maker) 55

scarab beetles 80, *80*, 92, 110, 115

scorpion-charmers 55, 56, 110, 124, 177, 184

scorpions 10, 110–11, *111*, 115, 122–23, 185, *185*

seasons 90

secrecy 18, 19–20

Sekhmet 87, 99; animal form 88, 102; demon days 167–68; demons unleashed by 90, 91; medical complaints and 53, 55, 90, 117; priests of 117, 124

sem-priests 44, 50, *52*, 53, 159

Serapis *185*
Serket 110
Seth 177; Aa-pehty praying to Seth *94*; The Contendings of Horus and Seth 127; demon days 91; healing spells 126; hippo symbol 95; and Horus 121; human and animal forms 86; murder of Osiris 122; myths 21, 23; pigs 115
'Seth animal' 95
Setne: Book of Thoth 44–50, *47*, 60, 64, 127; Duat 83; Tabubu 145; the underworld 66–67, 68, 71
Sety I, King 95, 174
Sety II, King 95
Seven Hathors 163
sex 139, 141, 142, *144*, 145, 146, 148
shabti-figures 96
shen knot 34
shesheshat (musical instrument) 144
shrewmouse 146
shrines, memorial 71–72
Siena Cathedral 186, *187*
Sirius 175, 178
sleep 163–66, 174
'smiting scene' *30*
snakes 9, 10, 92, *98*, 105–10, 115, 130, 155, 185; cobras 7, 72, 105, 121; venom 123
Snefru 43
Sobek 106, *109*, 110
solar eclipse 178
sorcerer-princes 44–50
speech, act of 13
spells 18, 192; against miscarriage 149; Book of the Dead 64; childbirth 151, 153; curses 24–29; handbook of 115; healing 24, 25, 116–17, 119, 122–23, 126, 129, 184;

knots and 31; love spells 141, 144; *mwtw* 72, 73; nightmares, dreams 165–66; against demons 90, 91; Pyramid Texts 61; water spells 141
sphinx 102, 163, 192
spirits 90; ancestral spirits 70–71; malevolent spirits 72–73; spirits of the dead 70–74
staffs *102*, 105
stars 175–80
stelae *94*, *103*, 106, *107*, *118*, 119–23, *120*, 151, *171*
Stoker, Bram 189
supernatural beings 67, 86–93
suppositories 128

Ta-Miaw 101
Tabubu 49, 64, 145
Tait 149
Taweret 88, 90, 109, 151, *152*
temples 50–51, 53, 184; birth-houses *160*, 161; rites 51, 53; scribal schools 61; sleeping quarters 166, 174
territories 25–26
Teti, King 17, 25
Thebes 131
Theosophy 188–89
Thoth 87, 164, 182; animal forms 7, 88; Book of 46, 47, 48–50, 60, 127; demon days 168; Hermes the Three-Times-Great 186; ibises and 112, *113*; Metternich Stela 121, 123; secret chambers of 44, 57; solar eclipse 178; temple of 135
Thutmose IV, King 163
tilapia 142
tjehenet (faience) 56
tombs 7; equipping 66, 67;

prayers and offerings to the spirit *82*, 83
Trajan, Emperor 131
trampling 29, 31
tusks, birth 156–57, *156–57*
Tutankhamun 22, *35*, 79, 96, *97*
Tutu *62–63*, 103, *103*, 105
'Two-Dog Palette' *93*
tyet knot 21, 22, 33–34, 56, 80

Unas, King 14, *15*, *16*
the underworld 66–70, 74, 83, 175
'Underworld Books' 68
uraeus 72, 105
urine, medical use of 129–30
Ursa Major *108*, 109–10, 175

vases: curse texts 27–28; letters to the dead 73
Venus 177
vultures 105, 112, 121

wab-priests 53, 55
wabet (embalming tent) 77
Wadjet *104*, 105, 121, 168
wands 9, 10, 95, *102*, 105, 156–57, *156–57*
was-sceptres 115
wax figures 12, 14, 28
wedjat-eyes 56, 121–22, *121*
Wepwawet 96
wet nurses 158
wings 113, 115
women: and magic 136; midwives 136, 153, 159; protection of 90; wise 56–57
words, magic 13–39
wormwood 128
writing 13, 17–19, 164

zodiac 177, 178–80, *179*, 181